ADVANCE PRAISE

"*Taking a Detour* is one of those must reads! Dave really hits home with his journey of the ups and downs with his battle to get his life back to normal. It is a moving testimonial of just how much fight we all have within ourselves to overcome adversity. No one should have to go through what Dave went through. Like me, you will probably be able to relate first hand to *Taking a Detour*."

> — Johnny Holliday, play by play broadcaster for the University of Maryland Terrapins and the Mid Atlantic Sports Network.

"Dave Sandler has helped his community navigate the challenges of detours, rush hours and crowded roads. Now in *Taking a Detour* he shares not only the story of how he came to do that, but also how he navigated life's greatest detours- a near death experience as well as other life threatening illnesses- and emerged with a new lease on life. And through that, Dave inspires us with valuable life lessons."

> — Ronald M. Shapiro, *The New York Times* best selling author and Chairman Shapiro Negotiations Institute, Attorney.

TAKING A DETOUR

**Life Lessons from a Near-Death Experience
and the Long Journey Back**

TAKING A DETOUR

Life Lessons from a Near-Death Experience and the Long Journey Back

Dave Sandler

with Dorrie Anshel

Apprentice House
Loyola University Maryland
Baltimore, Maryland

First Edition

Printed in the United States of America

Hardcover ISBN: 978-1-62720-082-0
Paperback ISBN: 978-1-62720-083-7
E-book ISBN: 978-1-62720-084-4

Design: Apprentice House
Editorial Development: Caroline Tell
Editing: Karl Dehmelt
Cover Photo: David Stuck

Published by Apprentice House

Apprentice House
Loyola University Maryland
4501 N. Charles Street
Baltimore, MD 21210
410.617.5265 • 410.617.2198 (fax)
www.ApprenticeHouse.com
info@ApprenticeHouse.com

*For Uncle Morris, who passed away
just as the first draft was being completed.
His unwavering faith in me
took Detour Dave to new heights.
I love you, miss you and thank you.*

CONTENTS

FOREWORD

Life is a journey, and no one knows that better than "Detour Dave" Sandler. It's not only his daily calling as a well-known and respected traffic reporter in Baltimore, it is the story of his life. And in this book he provides a guide to all of us that shows the strength he brings every day to his personal journey with cancer, his family, and his work. The challenges have been many and with grit, guts, determination and most of all the love of those around him Dave tells a story that will inspire us all.

No one chooses to hear the words, "You have cancer." None of us is ever prepared for what that means, or what the impact will be on our daily lives and our future. And especially, no young man at the very beginning of his adulthood wants or expects the interruption that cancer brings to the promise of a new stage in life, to the beginning of a career, to discovering love and starting a family.

That is exactly what happened to Dave Sandler. A young man of 20 years—still in college--and he found a lump, had a biopsy, and was told he had Hodgkin's disease. It was in the 1970's, a time when we were just beginning to have success in the treatment of some forms of cancer. Fortunately, Hodgkin's disease was one of those successes, and Dave was one of the early beneficiaries of what we had learned about cancer care. It wasn't easy, and it wasn't simple, but there was hope, and hope became the very definition of David's life.

A fulfilling marriage blessed with two beautiful children, a loving, caring and supportive wife, a devoted family, a well-known media figure in the Baltimore market—all the trimmings of success in life and in the community where he grew up. But danger was lurking, a danger possibly made worse by the very cancer treatment that saved his life. The tragedy appeared one day while playing softball and became another daunting challenge that Dave had to overcome, a challenge he never expected. Yet overcome it he did. His will to move forward, to succeed, to beat the odds are inspirational to those who read this book.

Detour Dave was one of my early patients after starting my oncology practice in 1977. It is now almost 40 years later, and we still have much to learn about caring for patients with cancer. Back then we were grateful when someone responded well to our new forms of treatment. Today, although we have made considerable progress in cancer care, we continue our search to find better drugs, find better combinations of drugs, and reduce the immediate side effects of the treatments we offer our patients. More important, as reflected in Dave's story, we also are paying more attention to the long term effects of our treatments, particularly for our young children and young adults faced with a cancer diagnosis. Finding a cure is no longer the sole goal of cancer treatment.

As Dave's story so vividly portrays, it's not just the number of days but the quality of those days that count. And despite the detours and the roadblocks, the incredible spirit of optimism as described in this book is a story that can inspire all of us, cancer survivors and those without cancer alike.

There are few among us who can recount a journey with cancer from young adulthood through five decades of life. Detour Dave is among those fortunate few. There are fewer still who can recount what it means to be a cancer survivor, to face the challenges that life and illness bring upon us sometimes relentlessly. His story and his message remind us of those early days of optimism, and the continuing days of hope and inspiration.

Dave's story is a story for all of us, for those who have had a personal experience with cancer, for those who have loved and cared for someone with cancer, for those whose journeys have been successful, and for those who remember someone who faced the disease with courage and dignity. It is a story of human spirit and humanity itself, of calling on our inner selves with a strength we frequently never knew we had, a will to keep on going, to keep on living, to keep on enjoying even the small moments that make life so special.

Most of all, this book is a testimonial not just to one person but to all those for whom he speaks. They are the survivors, they are the patients, they are our loved ones, our families, our friends, our colleagues, our communities. Through his voice and through his words, Dave Sandler brings hope and inspiration to many, every day. His book continues that noble mission.

— J. Leonard Lichtenfeld | Deputy Chief Medical Officer
American Cancer Society, Inc.

INTRODUCTION

I've spent my entire career delivering traffic and weather "on the 5's" for Baltimore's premier AM radio news station, WBAL, and its naughty kid brother, FM' s 98 ROCK. Faithful listeners tune in to hear "Detour Dave" warn them about overturned tractor trailers on I-95 south and six-car pile-ups on the beltway's Inner Loop. They count on me to make their rush-hour commutes a little less stressful; to get them to their destinations safely, even if it takes just a little longer than usual.

The words I use every day – roadblock, lane closure, accident – perfectly describe so much of what we all go through simply living our lives. There we are, cruising along at a comfortable speed, when *WHAM!*—something in the blind spot hits us hard. Beyond the moment of impact, there's the shock of realizing that our life plan has been upended in ways we never could have imagined.

Guiding listeners through unplanned routes is an apt metaphor for my own life. I didn't expect a cancer diagnosis at 20. I couldn't have anticipated dropping dead on a softball field 28 years later – and, thank goodness, coming back to tell the tale. Yet those unforeseen experiences have given my life renewed purpose and meaning. They taught me that if we're smart enough, we come to understand that every ending really is a new beginning—if we're lucky enough, we get multiple chances to redirect our lives for the better. I can't speak to the smart part, but I know for sure that I am one extremely lucky guy.

I decided to put into words what those near-death episodes, and lots of other detours before and after, have taught me. Accepting the stop and go. Embracing the detours. Always, always moving forward. In spite of them, or maybe because of them, I choose to live every day with optimism, confidence, and a willingness to go where unknown roads lead me.

Do I waver? Sure. Do I ask, "Why me?" Hey, I'm only human. But after everything I have been through, I trust in the possible. I truly enjoy each mile on the journey and believe that I'll make it to where I want to go. I hope that reading this book will help you see that even the scariest detours can have amazing outcomes.

DETOUR

1. MY BIGGEST DETOUR

Detour: To take an alternate route. To follow another path when one is blocked. To move away from what is ordinary and go in another direction.

August 9, 2009, was the most unexpected, terrifying day of my life. It was the day I almost died, and the biggest detour I've ever taken.

It was a typical summer Sunday morning in Baltimore, hot and steamy with the blinding sun feeling that much hotter on the unshaded softball field. A few dozen guys from all walks of life were sweating it out for the league championship. It was a friendly, yet intense, rivalry, and no one was working harder for that playoff spot than I was.

I danced around 2nd base waiting for my chance to advance. When the hitter behind me lined a single through the middle, I broke for third. I saw the center fielder bobble the ball, so I put my head down and dashed toward home to score the winning run.

As I rounded third, I remember feeling dizzy. That was the last thing I remember. According to everyone who saw what unfolded, I made it to home plate, then staggered and collapsed, hitting my head on the fence that protected the field from the dugout. I was out cold, but at that point no one knew why—or the severity of the underlying cause.

My teammate, Dr. Jan Katzen, screamed for his brother, Dr. Scott Katzen, an interventional cardiologist who happened to be in the stands that morning. Talk about being in the right place at the right time. Scott and my softball manager, Dr. Mike Herr, ran to where I lay unconscious. Scott saw immediately that I had stopped breathing and had no pulse. My color was ashen, and foam was coming out of my mouth.

I was dead.

SECTION 1 ➤

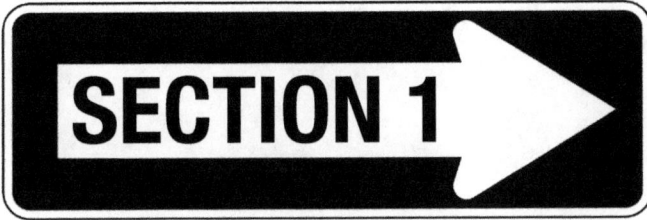

NEW ROADS TO TRAVEL

ORIOLE

2. FROM BASEBALL TO BROADCASTING 101

The moment I stepped onto a baseball field for the first time, I knew that I was destined to play pro ball when I grew up. Being a professional athlete is a dream for many young boys, but I believed that I had a real shot at "The Show." Fielding and throwing a guy out, hitting a clutch base hit, and striking out a batter came naturally to me. Defense, offense, it didn't matter. At age 10, playing for the Wellwood Little League, coaches and teammates told me I was the best player in the entire league. It may have been a small pond, but at that tender age it was my universe, and I loved being the biggest fish. I was confident that I would one day wear the orange and black jersey of my beloved Baltimore Orioles.

I continued playing on school and league teams through middle and high school and was certainly a top-notch player. In 10th grade I led off and played center field. But by my senior year in high school I could no longer figure out all the pitchers, and the curve ball left me swinging wildly for 9 out of 10 at-bats. As it typically happens—except in the rare cases of truly gifted athletes—the talent pool expanded and my elite status contracted. With college on the horizon, it was obvious that no scout would show up at my door with a fat scholarship offer; I simply wasn't good enough to compete at that level. So much for being signed to the O's.

It was disappointing, but I've never been the kind of person who falls apart when I have to take a sudden detour – I start devising a new game plan. I thought, "OK, if I can't *play* baseball for a living, I can stay connected through broadcasting. The next best thing to being on the field is watching and talking about the action. I know I can do that!" Becoming an announcer became my new goal, and the University of Maryland at College Park was the place to reach it. I declared as a Radio and TV Major. It sounded like fun, and a great way to start heading toward my career.

It was easy to find inspiration for a life in broadcasting. During my Little League days in the late 1960's, few games were televised. Radio was the only way to follow the Orioles, and there was only one voice in Baltimore baseball: the great Chuck Thompson. I listened to Chuck on a little transistor radio tucked into my shirt pocket, white earphone in my right ear. I'd never met him, of course, but he felt like a close friend. Whether I was cutting the lawn, riding my bike on a lazy summer afternoon, or staying up past my bedtime, Chuck's smooth tone and brilliant play-by-play transported me to Memorial Stadium where my idols competed.

No one painted a more vivid, exciting picture than Chuck. His voice was so warm, yet he would go crazy when Brooks Robinson made a spectacular diving catch at third or Boog Powell powered a ball over the outfield wall. Ask any Baltimorean of a certain age to quote Chuck's signature phrases and you'll hear, "Go to war Miss Agnes!" and "Ain't the beer cold?" If I couldn't be on the field, *that* was the guy I wanted to be: the guy in the booth bringing the game to life.

Besides having Chuck as a role model, I got an early introduction to broadcasting through Citizens' Band, or CB, radios, which were extremely popular when I was in elementary school. For those of you too young to remember, CB radios were an essential companion to long-distance truckers. As they carried cargo down lonely stretches of interstate highway, truckers would warn each other about accidents ahead or "Smokeys" waiting to issue speeding tickets, recommend friendly places to stop for a bite, or just talk to stay awake.

In 1975, country singer C.W. McCall released a song called "Convoy" that hit it big on the country and pop charts. The song, with its slang-filled conversation among three truckers, helped start the craze for CB radios with the general public. Everyone was creating "handles," on-air nicknames to identify themselves when they tuned in to an open frequency. My handle was – what else – "The Baltimore Oriole."

I remember plugging in my CB and mic and hanging my antenna off the balcony outside my bedroom window. The signal was powerful enough to reach people as far as 50 miles away. Discussing the O's latest performance and getting positive feedback from people I didn't know gave me tremendous confidence. I was just a kid, but I felt important and respected. It was a thrill when someone said, "Hey, it's the Baltimore Oriole! How you doin' tonight?" That recognition gave me my first taste of local celebrity, and I liked being a big shot, even if it my audience was only two or three other CB'ers. Now, all these years later, I'm doing the same thing on a larger scale – and getting paid for it.

I'm sure that all of us can point to formative experiences that lit the fire inside of us and led us to exactly where we were meant to be. These experiences don't have to be monumental to be life-changing; something as simple as a hobby or a trusted voice can teach us crucial lessons about who we are.

Sometimes we start on a particular path only to discover that we aren't quite as gifted as our parents (or coaches) tell us we are. Sometimes we've been inspired to go in a certain direction but don't realize it until years pass. Getting to where we're supposed to be is rarely a straight line. There are moments and people in our lives that help us change course when our original plans don't come to fruition.

So what if I wasn't good enough to pursue baseball professionally? That detour never deterred me from trying to find a career where I could excel. I don't know about you, but I'd much rather be great at my second choice than mediocre at my first.

To make it in any field, you must be honest with yourself about your chances for success given your skill set. Today, when I meet young people interested in a career in broadcasting, I give them three simple rules to consider:

- Make sure it's your passion because it's highly competitive.

- Make sure you have the raw talent and develop it to the fullest.

- If you discover it's not for you, keep searching until you find the path that makes the most of your gifts.

Passion sometimes is enough to elevate you into the top tier, if you're willing to grind it out and sacrifice everything else. But for most of us mortals, passion without the talent to fuel it is wasted energy. You'll ultimately find greater satisfaction doing a job you love – and one for which you have a gift – than to strike out repeatedly. This isn't to suggest that anyone should abandon his or her dreams – I encourage everyone to take their best shot. However, above all I'm a realist, and I know from a life filled with detours that we have to be open to change. No matter how hard I swung for the fences I wasn't cut out for the dugout. But that realization led me to a very happy and successful career choice.

I still wear my orange and black jersey – in the stands or in front of the TV. The last time I was on a baseball field was a personal triumph, but of a very different kind. When I'm behind the mic I often think of Chuck Thompson and the standard of excellence he set. I owe him a debt of gratitude. And while my CB radio hasn't seen any action for decades, I'm proud that Detour Dave has become my handle—but in my mind, I'll always be the Baltimore Oriole!

AMBITION

3. EARLY DAYS BEHIND THE MIC

Once I settled in at College Park I began meeting other Radio and Television majors in class and around campus. I soon learned that anyone enrolled in the major could audition for a position at the student-run campus radio station, WMUC. I was excited at the prospect of working at a real radio station, even if it was only 10 watts and reached an audience of a few thousand. This was an opportunity to find out quickly whether I had any talent as a broadcaster. I'd already given up on one dream career and I didn't have another back-up plan. This had to work.

I walked in to the station nervous but hopeful. My try-out went well and I was soon behind the mic a few hours a week announcing sports results. Writing and talking about all the sports I loved, particularly Terps football and basketball, was a real thrill, not to mention a huge step up from my days as the "Baltimore Oriole." I'd had more air time reporting from my bedroom, but the quality of my work improved tremendously at WMUC.

The experience gave me a real taste of what was required to be a reporter and on-air presence, and I loved it. I continued at the station until graduation, by which time I'd amassed a considerable number of hours behind the mic. It was a fun and wonderful introduction to what I hoped would be my long-term career. But first I had to find a job in one of the lowest-paying, most highly competitive fields. Not a fun prospect, but I was willing to do what it took to land that first job.

With diploma in hand and a stack of crisp resumes on my desk, my job search began in earnest. This was in the days before computers, social media connections or even a Craigslist help wanted section. The Sunday paper and the college placement center were the only options back in 1983, unless you had a personal connection. I didn't know anyone in the industry at that point, so I couldn't depend on contacts. Landing a job was entirely up to me.

There I sat, day after day, with the phone, the pile of resumes, envelopes and stamps. Whoever said finding a job is a full-time job had it right. I cannot count the number of resumes I mailed out. Then there were the dreaded follow-up calls. The most frequent response, by phone and letter, was, "We appreciate your interest in (Company Name). Unfortunately, there is nothing available at this time, but we will keep your resume on file for future opportunities." I heard that rejection so many times I could recite it in forwards and backwards in my sleep.

Finally, after nine months of calling, mailing, interviewing and following up, I landed a part-time job at WCBM, an AM station in Baltimore that features news, sports and talk. When I describe the job as part-time, I'm being generous. It was three hours a week answering listeners' calls and putting them on the air for a talk show called "Colts Final." The show aired on Sundays following each just-completed Colts game (this was when the Colts belonged to Baltimore, not Indianapolis; many die-hard fans say they always will, but that's fodder for a different book). It may not have been much, but for a die-hard sports fan like me, it was the best first job I could have imagined. My foot was firmly in the door, and that's all the encouragement I needed to keep working my way up.

Like many companies, WCBM preferred to hire from within. I frequently checked the in-house help wanted board hoping that a more permanent position had opened up. After a few months with "Colts Final" a full-time job posting appeared: Desk Assistant WCBM Radio News. Hours: 4 a.m.-12 Noon. I had no idea what a Desk Assistant did; the hours were brutal, but I wanted that job more than anything. Oh, and did I mention that it paid a whopping $8,000 a year? Even by 1983's standards that was a poverty wage. But it was full-time. I would have eaten dog food for that job.

They gave me the job partially because I begged and largely because no sane person wanted those crazy hours. I woke up at 3 a.m., drove to the news room and did pretty much anything off-air they asked me to. My main responsibility was to record segments for later airplay, including phone interviews with newsmakers, the day's forecast from the AccuWeather service, and network news feeds. There was a fair amount of grunt work as well, but I approached every task, no matter how small, like it was vital to the mission. Waking up that early was inhuman, but I was young and ambitious; my colleagues were terrific, and the environment was fast-paced.

Some months passed. As much as I enjoyed and appreciated the job, I craved being an on-air personality. I had learned so much and I believed that I could do it. Unfortunately, there were no openings at News/Talk 68. I put out some casual feelers at other local stations, hoping that I wouldn't have to wait too much longer to move up to the next level.

One of those inquiries paid off quickly. The AccuWeather forecaster, a nice guy named Elliott Abrams, delivered weather casts to hundreds of stations around the country. One early morning after we'd finished recording, I asked him if he knew of any stations looking for on-air talent. I guess it was meant to be, because he had just learned that WRSC/97 Quick in State College, Pennsylvania, had an opening.

As soon as I left work for the day I mailed them a resume and cover letter. They responded within a few days, and as fast as that, I was driving north on Route 322 to "Happy Valley," home of the Nittany Lions.

The interview went so well that they offered me the position on the spot. The station was an AM/FM combo that aired news, sports and music, and they wanted me to handle all three. I was dying to say yes, but I needed to know if I could afford to take the job. I was willing to start at the bottom, but I simply couldn't relocate for a pay cut. When the station manager told me the salary was $12,500 a year, you better believe I grabbed it. That was a 50% raise, and, in 1984, a decent sum of money for a young, single guy.

WRSC wanted me to start right away, so I gave notice and my heartfelt thanks to the team at WCBM. I will never forget that experience and the wonderful people who taught me how to make a radio show hum, both on and off the air. They helped me gain the confidence to want more for myself and to believe that I could make it behind the mic.

With a start date looming, my next step was to find a place to live and some half-decent furniture. My dad drove to PA with me, and we found a beautiful one-bedroom apartment in a great area right around the corner from the radio station. It was a perfect second job and an incredibly lucky break. With just a year or so of experience I had landed an amazing opportunity on the air for significantly more money.

I loved getting up and going to work every day. I played some music, read the local and national news, and honed my on-air vocal skills. As a bonus, the station sent me to cover Penn State sporting events and let me deliver some of those stories on air. If someone had asked me to describe my dream job, that was it.

Except for one thing: a girl named Jody-- who was back in Baltimore.

We had met just before I landed the job in PA, and I really cared for her. Not to sound like a dinosaur, but this was in the days before cell phones, so every call was "long distance" and expensive. Over the next six months I drove back to Baltimore practically every weekend to see her, and that six-hour round-trip drive was grueling. The more we saw each other, the more I missed her – it was definitely getting serious. That meant either she was coming north to be with me or I was heading back to Baltimore.

Jody is a twin; like most twins, she shares a special bond with her sister, Alisa. She's also extremely close to her older sister, Nancy, and to her extended family. It was clear that she wasn't leaving Charm City. I faced a terrible dilemma: dream job or dream girl? It was no contest. Jody took it in the first round.

On the professional side, those six months in PA were enough to convince me that I could make it on the air in any market. With stronger industry connections and solid experience behind me, jobs were easier to find. Within days of launching my search in the Baltimore area I found a job in Bel Air, MD at WHRF-AM. It was a similar position with comparable pay to the one in State College. I could be with Jody *and* do the work that I loved! In short order I had to say goodbye again to a team of professionals I liked and admired. I owe them a debt of gratitude for giving me my first on-air shot and preparing me to take the next step in my career.

I settled in at WHRF and got into the rhythm of delivering news, weather and playing music. I liked the station and wasn't looking to make another change anytime soon. But you know how that goes: when you're not looking, opportunity finds you.

After a few months on the air I got a call from a recruiter who had heard my show and wondered if I'd be interested in doing on-air traffic reports for a company called Metro Traffic Control. Honestly, I didn't know anything about that end of the business. Since I took back roads to work at off hours, I rarely paid attention to radio traffic reports. I declined the offer and went on doing my thing for a few more months.

Then, talk about the unexpected: I came to work as usual and was told my services were no longer needed. I don't recall ever getting a clear reason for my dismissal, but when you're out, you're out. I packed my desk and left, bewildered but resigned to starting the job search again. On the drive home I ran through my mental address book and remembered the recruiter who had contacted me about doing traffic reports. I thought, "If they're still interested in me, I'm interested in them. I know I can learn whatever they need me to do." I was pretty sure I'd written down his name somewhere and finally found it scribbled on a notepad in my box of personal effects.

I wasted no time calling David Sapperstein, Metro's president, and he was pleasantly surprised to hear from me. To my relief, the job was open. If hired, I would deliver traffic reports to multiple stations from Metro's offices in downtown Baltimore. I was intrigued. I had no idea about how to do it or what it was supposed to sound like, but I was game to try.

David liked my voice and casual on-air demeanor. He said I came across as friendly and approachable, which was essential for consistently delivering unpleasant news – if you've ever been stuck in Baltimore's notorious daily back-ups, you understand what he meant. "People tune in to hear solid information about how to commute with minimal hassle," he said. "You have to be credible, professional and helpful. I think you have what it takes. Interested?"

I needed a job, and he was persuasive. How could I say no? To prepare, I started listening exclusively to traffic reports on every radio station that broadcast them. I wanted to understand the pacing, cadence and tone in order to incorporate those qualities into my own delivery. Once I committed, I was in 100% and was determined to be the best traffic reporter on the air.

I was lucky to have a generous mentor at Metro, Tom Olson. Tom had the same polished, melodic tone and effortless delivery of my idol, Chuck Thompson. No matter how bad the crash or how long the delay, Tom could immediately put drivers at ease. His voice was calm, trustworthy and believable. That's how I wanted to sound.

I listened. I mimicked. I may have been the new guy on the beat, but I rehearsed until I sounded like I'd been doing the job for years. I guess David Sapperstein saw something in me that I didn't see in myself, and I am forever grateful to him for helping me take such a career changing detour.

GRATITUDE

4. INTRODUCTION TO TRAFFIC

My time with Metro Traffic was fast-paced and an unbelievably rich training ground. I learned the lingo that made my reports creative, ear-catching and informational. Tom Olson's delivery set a high bar, so I tried to copy his techniques while carving out a distinctive sound. My personality is laid back and calm, and that's how I wanted listeners to feel: "Yes, this is serious, but we can get through the backup together. No need to stress."

I reported traffic for a number of stations, including WBAL Radio, the powerful 50,000-watt news/talk station that dominates Baltimore's AM dial. Several times each day, I broadcasted the backups, accidents and construction plaguing drivers on the beltway, side roads and tunnels. Metro Traffic was getting positive feedback about my reports, and I felt that I'd found a fulfilling career; I preferred traffic reporting to hosting a music show and assumed I'd be at Metro for as long as I wanted.

About nine months into my tenure, David called me in to his office, a serious look on his face. He told me that one of his major clients had requested that Metro add a female voice to the reporting team. My services, while excellent, were no longer needed; there simply was not enough room for me and this new full-time hire. However, he wanted to know if I would be willing to stay on and train her.

His proposition took a second to digest. I had just lost my job, but could keep it until my replacement was groomed for the air— kind of like sharpening the axe for your executioner. It was surreal, but I agreed to do it for several reasons: first, it would give me a financial cushion while I looked for something else. Second, I didn't want to burn any bridges, because it was likely that I'd need a reference in the coming weeks. If I played ball with David on this, perhaps he'd play ball with me?

That evening, after my shift, I started making calls to other stations around town. My first was to BAL. They knew my work and were the big player in the market, so I figured I'd start at the top. I told them that Metro was making some changes and I found myself suddenly available. The response was overwhelmingly positive, and they invited me to interview that week. I was gratified, but didn't learn until I went in *why* they were so eager to talk to me.

When I arrived for the meeting I couldn't believe my eyes: There was Tom Clendening, a former co-worker of mine at WCBM and now the News Director at BAL. The radio fraternity is small, but how lucky was I to be meeting with someone I knew and genuinely liked? We hugged hello and Tom kicked off the discussion with an unexpected question: "Dave, have you ever been up in a small plane?"

"How small?" I asked.

"A two-seater."

I said, "They make them that small?"

We had a laugh, but he was serious. He said, "We've been listening to you report for us on Metro Traffic Control and really like your style. We want to start our own independent traffic service, and we can't think of a better person than you to head it up.

"There is a little twist, however. We want someone to go up in a plane and report the traffic live, directly from the air, both mornings and afternoons. Are you game?"

Here was another twist, and I had to think fast. I was thrilled and a little intimidated by their up-in-the-air approach. My head told me that I'd be crazy to take the risk. My heart told me I'd be crazy not to grab this exciting opportunity with both hands and hang on for the ride. As usual, my heart won. It took all of two seconds to say, "Sure, I can handle that!" I tried not to show my eagerness, but I'm sure my voice squeaked just a little.

The position was beyond anything I had expected. I was certain the offer couldn't get any sweeter until Tom slid an envelope across the desk and told me to look inside. Like the scene in *Moneyball,* where Red Sox owner John Henry offers Billy Beane $12.5 million to be the team's GM, I gingerly opened the flap and peeked at the figure on the paper. It was $25,500 per year, more than twice what I had earned at any job. I couldn't sit still another second. I jumped up and high-fived him, my smile stretched from ear to ear. I accepted on the spot. This was one of the best days of my life. My first thought was to call Jody with the news. She went nuts.

With my exit from Metro and my BAL start date just weeks away, I continued training David's new hire. I gave it my all, but didn't feel that she was making sufficient progress; apparently David agreed with my assessment. After three weeks of intensive coaching he let her go. She hadn't delivered a single report.

Now for plot twist number three: he offered me my job back.

I was stunned. I composed myself and reminded him that I had committed to BAL and, as much as I appreciated the offer, could not accept. He paused thoughtfully then responded tersely, "Dave, if you leave, I'll sue you." Plot twist number four.

As a condition of employment, I had signed a non-compete agreement, which prohibited me from taking a traffic job with another organization for two years after leaving the company. I understood why David required the agreement. He'd built a successful business and had a virtual monopoly in the market. He nurtured the on-air talent and created the reporting infrastructure. He wanted to protect his investment, and the clause signaled no poaching to potential competitors or jumping ship to other employers.

While I understood the rationale, this put me in a terrible bind. I had a better job waiting and couldn't imagine continuing at Metro, given the circumstances around my firing and rehiring. I asked him if he would consider voiding the contract in this extraordinary situation. He declined, citing the unhealthy precedent it would set. If he made one exception … he was sure I understood his position. He pointed out that my departure meant a double hit to the business because he was losing me *and* the lucrative BAL contract. He made it perfectly clear that he would sue me for breach of contract if I left.

I told him I'd think it over and walked out of his office extremely disappointed, certain that the biggest professional opportunity of my life was already a memory. I also had to acknowledge that I might soon be unemployed, period.

I called Tom to deliver the bad news, certain he'd say, "Sorry Dave, but we just can't take on a legal fight over this." To my relief, station management rallied around me. The station's lawyer read the agreement and determined that it was too broadly written to be enforceable. BAL wanted me, and would not back down until they'd tried to work it out with David. I went live from the skies over Baltimore in December of 1986 while we waited for a final disposition. About a year later, a judge concurred that the contract was not enforceable, and the dispute was put to rest. I've been at BAL ever since.

My relationship with David remained cordial, despite all the crazy convolutions (I never asked, but I'm guessing that he had a serious conversation with his attorneys about tightening up that clause). He never heard a negative word from me and I never uttered a negative word about him. That's not to say that I accepted his refusal without some resentment. It took tremendous self-control to stay calm when David threatened to sue. I'd been fired and had a better opportunity waiting. Knowing that he had the power to derail my career was infuriating. I felt that I'd gone above and beyond to help Metro, so a clean exit would have been preferable.

Nonetheless, I acknowledge that he had a point. My leaving had the potential to open the floodgates and ruin his enterprise. That insight made it possible, even easy, for me to hold my tongue. Empathy is a powerful tool; I encourage you to use it – and if that doesn't work, hire a good attorney.

LUCKY

5. UP, UP AND AWAY

With the lawsuit settled and BAL's station management eager to get the new traffic service underway, it was time to climb into the plane and head skyward.

I had never flown in a small plane, so I had no idea how small "small" could be. Picture a clown car, the tiniest vehicle imaginable, from which a dozen or more garishly painted humans and their over-sized shoes emerge. I'm not exaggerating when I say that the plane might have had even less head, arm and leg room. Two seats were jammed together with a shoebox-sized compartment behind them for one tiny carry-on bag. My trusty pilot Zoran and I squeezed in shoulder-to-shoulder – we must have looked like conjoined twins. I'm surprised there was room for the oxygen we needed to breathe.

Zoran was a Swedish flight instructor with a heavy accent, but I came to understand his lingo quickly, and we hit it off from our first flight together. As you can imagine, he and I got to know each other pretty well, down to the brand of toothpaste we used. Yes, it was that intimate.

The passenger seat of the Cessna 152 became my airborne office for three hours every morning and two and half hours each afternoon,

Monday through Friday. I delivered traffic reports every 10 minutes to WBAL and its FM sister station, 98 ROCK. The excitement of soaring over downtown Baltimore more than compensated for the lack of space. Seeing the development of so many construction projects, the lush landscape around the beautiful mansions of Guilford and Roland Park, and, of course, watching the toy-sized cars stopping and starting around the Beltway, zipping through the Fort McHenry and Harbor Tunnels and meander down the JFX. It was fascinating from my bird's eye perch, and I often found myself lost in the moment. More than once, Zoran had to nudge me and nod toward the two-way radio so I wouldn't forget to report.

The weather was always the deciding factor as to whether or not we would fly. The plane was light, so too much wind or limited visibility was enough to ground us. There was drag and a headwind every day, of course, but on rougher days I'd emerge from the plane feeling as if I had sparred a few rounds with Muhammad Ali. Either my head would keep hitting the ceiling and my side would bang into the door, or my chest would strike the steering wheel because of the gusts. It was part of the job, so I just limped home and got ready to go up again.

Because there are two rush hours a day – although, some Baltimoreans might say it's rush hour 24/7 – the job required us to be in the air from 6-9 a.m. and again from 4-6:30 p.m. I got up at the ungodly hour of 4:30 a.m., drove to the airport, and went aloft until 9. As soon as we landed, I had seven hours of free time before I had to return to the airport and start over. I'm not complaining, believe me – it was the greatest job at the most popular station in a sizeable market, and I knew how lucky I was to have it. I'm sure that plenty of people would welcome a break in the middle of the day, and I was determined to make the most of every minute.

When I started the job, Jody was working, and our daughter Alix was a baby. I was fortunate to be home with her during a good part of the afternoon. I loved playing with her, feeding her, and just hanging with my girl. When she napped, sometimes I did, too. It was a great way to refresh before going airborne for the evening rush. No matter what was happening on the ground I had to be "on" when delivering my reports, and rising at 4:30 occasionally took its toll.

I guess you could say I was one of the early "Mr. Moms," running errands, doing the grocery shopping and laundry, and most importantly taking care of Alix. At the time it was untraditional, and I got a bit of teasing about it. I didn't mind. It's my nature to let things roll off my back, and I felt that having that time with my daughter was a gift that most men don't get. They had no idea what they were missing. The early bonds we built have kept us close through all the stages of her life, and I cherish the memories of our afternoons together.

Regardless of the physical discomfort and unusual schedule, I relished being up in that tiny plane reporting the traffic. The view was spectacular and gave me such a clear perspective on what was happening on the roads. Instead of looking at a single spot in isolation I saw the whole picture and could immediately convey to listeners what kind of jam they were heading into. I think that gave greater value to our reporting accuracy, and the surge in listeners proved that management had hatched a smart idea.

An unexpected highlight of the job was trading barbs with the on-air personalities, especially on 98 Rock. Unlike BAL, which had a serious, news-focused brand, 98 ROCK was the bad boy of the FM dial. The station played classic rock and had irreverent DJs behind the mic during the morning and afternoon rushes. They developed recognizable personalities known for their jokes and pranks. While my on-air persona was calm and reassuring, they constantly tried to pull me into the craziness. I had to be quick to keep up with them, and the verbal play kept me on my toes.

It was during one of those exchanges that I got my nickname, Detour Dave. All the credit for coining the memorable sign off, "Detour Dave, the 98 Rock Traffic Slave," goes to Chris Emry, a funny and very popular DJ. I thought it was brilliant and a worthy replacement for my first on-air persona, the Baltimore Oriole. The audience, who pictured me up in the plane in a leather bomber jacket, white silk scarf streaming behind me as I reported the perils of Baltimore traffic, thought it was hilarious. Little did I, or the stations, know how well that brand would serve us all in the coming years.

The nickname caught on so quickly and completely, people forgot my real name. When I made appearances on behalf of the station, people would say, "There goes Detour Dave!" I can't think of another traffic reporter who enjoyed as much recognition; I owe a huge debt to all the on-air personalities at BAL and 98 ROCK for making me an integral part of their shows.If station management had paid a brand development company hundreds of thousands of dollars, I doubt they would have come up with anything as clever or as spot on. My job was not just to warn listeners of back-ups, but to help them navigate through and around them. Bravo to Chris for creating a moniker that has resonated with listeners for close to 30 years.

DIVERSITY

6. BECOMING A DJ: AN UNEXPECTED TURN

Not long after my arrival at WBAL, newsman John Patti approached me about a part-time job with his company. "Oh no," I thought. "Here comes the network marketing pitch. How do I get out of this gracefully?" To my relief, he wasn't hawking vitamins or magnets—it was something completely different and unexpected: DJ'ing parties. Even though I was earning more than twice what I had at any previous job, I was always interested in stocking away more for the future. By this time, I had a house and Alix to support. A little extra money couldn't hurt.

John told me a bit about his company, The Music Pac. He employed quite a few others in the building and they really enjoyed it. They were busy every weekend running all sorts of affairs at different venues in the Baltimore metro area. He asked, "Have you ever DJ'd before?" I said, "You mean like on the radio? I've done a little bit of that." "No," he replied, "for weddings and anniversary parties, sweet-sixteens and Bar Mitzvahs." I'd certainly been to countless parties but had no clue about what was involved; frankly, music was not my thing. We agreed that observing him in action was the best way to see if I'd like it. I'd get a feel for everything involved in running a successful event – and there were plenty of details – and determine whether I had the talent and stamina to entertain a crowd for four to five hours.

Today the music is digital and the equipment is minimal. You walk in with the equivalent of a 5-lb. bag of flour and you're good to go. But in the mid-80s, DJs relied on multiple turntables and hundreds of 45 records, from Frank Sinatra to "Gonna Make You Sweat," from Motown to disco, plus the songs currently on the pop charts. And don't forget all the party anthems: "Cotton Eye Joe," "Hava Nagila," "YMCA," and "The Electric Slide," among others. The set up and tear down were exhausting grunt work that involved hauling over-sized milk crates filled with records, turntables, wires and microphones. If you were doing a kids' party, you also brought favors and game paraphernalia, which might include blow-up musical instruments, toilet paper, giant clown shoes, flashing rings and bracelets, glow sticks, hats, sunglasses, and other party-themed gear.

Despite the heavy load, once the party started it was tons of high-energy fun. I watched eagerly as John showed me how to manage a Saturday night wedding, from cueing up the songs to corralling guests for the cake cutting. He had a tried-and-true system and I was eager to learn it. John was so patient, and a great tutor. He was a wonderful entertainer with an innate sense of how to pace the evening so that everyone could shake it (or cha-cha) on the dance floor. Watching him gave me a clear sense of what was required to run a memorable party. He even trusted me enough to spin some records and make a few announcements that evening.

Of all the tips John gave me that night, one piece of advice resonates to this day: "Make sure you eat!" I looked puzzled, so he explained. If you're well fed and focused, you can give your all to making the party an unforgettable experience. If you're hungry, the fast pace will consume your energy. Your job is to satisfy your clients and to ingratiate yourself with the staff working the venue – not easy when you're ready to pass out from low blood sugar. So when aspiring DJs ask me how to guarantee that a party will rock, I tell them, "Get the names right and eat."

As the final notes of Donna Summer's "Last Dance" faded around 1 a.m., I thanked John for a great evening. I thought to myself, "This could be a fun way to spend a few Saturday nights a month while getting paid." We drove back to John's and started unloading all the equipment. There were about 10 other guys, all of whom worked for John, hanging out after their gigs. They helped us put away the crates as they compared notes. By now it was 2 a.m., and I was beat, so I said good-night. John graciously handed me some cash, and I headed home thinking, "I just landed a part-time job. I wonder if Jody would be willing to give up some Saturday nights so I could make some extra money?"

When I saw John at work the following Monday, I told him that I would love to learn more about being a mobile DJ. He was thrilled that I wanted to join The Music Pac and promised to put me on the roster for upcoming events. He employed two DJ's per party: the lead entertainer who helmed the mic and the helper. Of course I would start out as the latter. He assured me that as I gained more experience the money would get better – the helper earned $35 per gig – and eventually I would move up to be the lead man. He also told me that the attire for most events, especially weddings, was a tuxedo. I remember my first "monkey suit" so well: an all-black jacket and pants with a black vest with a signature gold bow tie. Baby, I was stylin'. With Jody's blessing, I started right away and quickly found my weekends booking up.

I was the helper to all sorts of characters; some were talkative and allowed me to jump right in while others were more protective of their lead status and gave me little latitude to assist with the party. I didn't mind. It was a blast going from glittering reception rooms to knotty, pine-paneled American Legion halls and everything in between. Some nights it was shrimp cocktail, others it was chips and dip. I just rolled with it, watching, listening, and learning. And I never forgot to eat.

About six months in, my pay escalated to $50-$60 per event. I'd never been the lead DJ but I was taking on more responsibility with each party. I had a feeling that I was getting close. One Saturday evening, John took me to a wedding at Martin's West, a large banquet facility with multiple locations throughout Baltimore. He was the headliner, of course, and I had no expectation that I'd be doing more than usual as his helper. Imagine how shocked I was when, at the end of the cocktail hour, he whispered, "You're on!" I replied, "What? You're joking." He said, "Dave, you're ready. You've been at this for months. You know the drill, so get out there and introduce the bride and groom."

I could feel my hands shaking and sweat forming on my upper lip and forehead. John was right, though. I'd watched the order of operations so often I knew exactly what to do. I reviewed the cheat sheet and ran a mental "movie" of how I'd seen all the other guys present the happy couple. Without thinking, I took the mic and proclaimed, "Everyone please rise. Now, for the first time as husband and wife, ladies and gentlemen, let's hear it for Mr. and Mrs. Smith!" The bride and groom entered the ballroom to thunderous cheers, and with that simple phrase my fear disappeared. The party was on and I was in charge.

For the rest of the evening, the music and announcements flowed smoothly, as if I'd been the lead DJ all my life. I looked over at John occasionally and saw him smiling. He was happy with my performance, and so was I. Being behind the mic in the plane or on the dance floor was equally comfortable and easy. I realized, too, that my calm on-air demeanor would serve me well in this new capacity as party emcee. Clients came into the events extremely nervous about everything being perfect; they needed to feel confident that the person they'd chosen to run the party could pull it off without a hitch. I understood that for most of my clients this was the biggest and most expensive night of their lives. They'd spent years saving for a celebration, and I wanted to be worthy of their trust. I vowed to work as hard as I could to become the best DJ on the party circuit.

At the close of that first reception, I presented our usual complimentary bottle of champagne to the newlyweds and spun the final record of the night. As I helped John pack up, I remember thinking that I'd climbed another rung on the professional ladder. How high could this new opportunity take me? I couldn't wait to find out.

After a few parties, being the lead entertainer was a snap. I gained so much confidence once it was my show. Even though I hadn't considered myself much of a music guy, I discovered that every party has a unique rhythm; I instinctively understood what songs should be sequenced to keep the crowd going. I loved being on the microphone directing traffic (sound familiar?) to the dance floor or the buffet tables, doing the introductions, and making sure all the evening's traditions were carried out flawlessly. At the same time, the client must always be the center of attention. My job is to facilitate, get out of the way, and let the party breathe. It works every time.

Of course, the DJ can't facilitate successfully without a great banquet team. We have to be in sync to ensure that the evening runs on schedule. That's why I always made it a point to develop good relationships with the banquet managers, bartenders, and wait staff at every venue. I got to know some incredibly dedicated, hard-working people who ran themselves ragged at event after event. I have tremendous respect for everyone in the catering/service industries. They spend their weekends lugging 100-pound trays with smiles on their faces, trying to keep the guests happy no matter what. Believe me, it's one of the toughest jobs on the planet.

One of the best teams I've had the pleasure of working with is the team at the Hunt Valley Golf Club. Known for its gorgeous setting, overlooking rolling hills and mature trees, the venue is popular with Baltimore brides. On one particular summer evening, the wedding ceremony and cocktail hour were held on the terrace. While her guests enjoyed hors d'oeuvres and drinks, the poor bride was stung by a bee. She ran up to me and said she had to leave for the emergency room immediately because she was highly allergic to bee stings. "I'll be back as soon as I can. Please don't let the guests know anything's wrong!" she said, and then she disappeared.

Now, I'm thinking, "I have to work in the introductions, first dance, toasts, cake cutting and bouquet toss without a bride. This is going to be tricky." I huddled with the banquet manager, and we came up with a game plan to serve dinner and start the dancing early, hoping that the bride would make it back in time to enjoy her own reception. The kitchen and servers had to hustle, but with a little juggling and hot tunes we kept the guests well fed and entertained. And yes, a very appreciative and healthy bride had her first dance and cut her cake. I'll never forget how quickly and calmly the Hunt Valley team responded to what could have been a disaster. When the entertainer and the staff work together to create a seamless event, no matter what calamity occurs, the clients go home happy.

John Patti got me started in a second career that has become a mainstay of my professional life. For that I am truly grateful. He fully expected that I'd go out on my own one day, and he let me fly. After a few years with The Music Pac, I established my DJ business, Traffic Jams, with a focus on weddings and Bar/Bat Mitzvahs. The Detour Dave brand gave the business a huge boost. People who heard me every day on the radio felt that they knew and trusted me. They loved having the traffic slave as their emcee, and the business grew quickly.

I've been facilitating celebrations since 1986, and I enjoy it as much today as I did when I was part of John's Music Pac. People often ask me, "How do you keep it fresh night after night?" The simple answer is that I treat every job as if it's my first; for the client, it is the first and perhaps only time they'll hold this event. I never forget that, and I never take for granted that the next job will be there. I strive to bring my A-game every time – my clients expect it, and I expect it of myself. I've been fortunate to work for some of Baltimore's most famous sports legends, including Cal Ripken, Ray Lewis, and Marvin

Lewis, formerly a Ravens defensive coach who is now head coach of the Cincinnati Bengals. It's an honor to have the trust of some of the most well-known names in the business, but to me every client is a VIP. No matter the occasion or budget, I do my utmost to create an evening they'll never forget.

Whether you're the president of a multi-national corporation, a small business owner, or the person who empties the wastebaskets, give your job and your colleagues the dignity and respect they deserve. Give yourself respect in equal measure. Take pride in what you do. There is honor in doing an honest day's work. Regardless of your responsibilities, be the best at them—no coasting, no excuses. When you do less than you're capable of it shows.

Of course, you have every right to be unhappy about your job; when that unhappiness affects your performance it's time to start looking. Remember, you are never entitled to disappoint people who count on you.

ENTREPRENEURSHIP

7. DETOUR DAVE, INC. BEGINS

The airborne traffic service was a solid hit for WBAL and the biggest part of my daily routine for the next several years. Pardon the pun, but I made the daily drive to and from Martin State Airport in Middle River, MD, on autopilot. I got up at the 4-o'clock hour, brushed my teeth, washed my face, threw on some sweats, and off I went for the 35-minute drive. I checked in with the station when I arrived, headed to the hangar to pre-flight the plane, hopped in with my new pilot, Mike Zachary, and away we went. Zoran had moved on to another job by then, so Mike took over the controls for me. It wasn't uncommon for private pilots, most of whom were primarily flight instructors, to grab other opportunities when they came along. Over the course of 15 years in the air I've had the pleasure of working with at least 10 pilots, including two of my favorites: the father/son duo of Buddy and Chip Gnau. Chip continues working with me to this day. He's a stellar guy and a terrific pilot.

In radio, it's common to round up a station's frequency on the dial for simplicity and for marketing purposes. WBAL was known as "Radio 11" since it was located at 1090 on the AM dial; the same was true of 98 ROCK, which was at 97.9 FM. I delivered traffic on

WBAL every 11 minutes to play off the Radio 11 nickname and every 15 minutes for 98 ROCK. On BAL it was a pretty straightforward proposition, in keeping with the station's brand as a news/talk outlet. Listeners tuned in for a detailed report so they could get to work with minimal delay.

98 ROCK was a completely different animal. The classic rock format attracted a young, hip, primarily male audience who expected to be entertained. They wanted their traffic reports served up with personality and humor, and I was encouraged to build on the Detour Dave persona. Once the nickname gained traction, the banter with the DJs became an integral part of each report; like them, I was creating a recognizable on-air presence.

It wasn't unusual for conversations to veer wildly off topic, especially when there was a guest in the studio. I'm not sure whether it was harder to control the plane or the DJs, but it was always a thrilling ride. From rock stars to porn stars, you never knew who would pop in for a guest spot, especially during morning drive time. When the DJs were on a roll, they weren't going to kill the momentum for the traffic report; I was expected to play off whatever thread they were pursuing, no matter how R-rated or infantile.

One of the most memorable incidents was with Mickey Cucchiella of the "Mickey and Amelia Morning Show." His guest was a scantily clad young woman from the adult entertainment industry named Jessie Jane. The weather was terrible that day, so the plane was grounded. Mickey called me into the studio and dared me to sit on Jessie's lap while I gave my traffic report. To throw me off my game, he instructed her to grind seductively and "give Dave your best action." He challenged me, "Dave, if you can get through your report without hesitating or any ***other*** difficulty (wink wink), you win." I sat down and, while everyone howled with laughter, I nailed it, just as I always did. Mickey was impressed. Jessie Jane was perplexed: apparently she was used to getting a reaction from her co-workers, but I didn't miss a beat. Now *that's* concentration.

Speaking of infantile pranks, I played my fair share of them. I will never forget the Thanksgiving that Chip and I ruined a rival station's holiday promotion, all in good fun. B-104 had launched a huge balloon from the 41st Street Bridge near TV Hill. Chip and I saw the balloon as we were looping around the beltway and decided to take a closer look. It was a giant turkey, complete with wattle, tail feathers, and a pilgrim's hat. Chip and I thought it would be hilarious if we knocked that giant turkey out of the sky. I happened to know B-104's afternoon DJ, a childhood friend named Larry Wachs, who has a superb sense of humor. I couldn't wait to hear his reaction as the bird plummeted toward the earth from its mighty perch above the Jones Falls Expressway.

We approached the flying fowl and punctured it with our propeller in a single pass. Down it went, a deflated brown and orange tangle of fabric—the once-majestic bird was no more. Larry joked about it for the next 15 minutes, cracking one lame bird joke after another. Our direct hit was a huge hit on the air for Detour Dave, 98 ROCK and B-104. Larry, Chip and I laugh about it to this day.

As Detour Dave grew in popularity, I became much more than a faceless name with a soothing voice. Both stations wanted me to represent them at events to help promote programming, and I was happy to do so. I made appearances at rock concerts and at sponsors' businesses. I started doing live and recorded commercials for advertisers. The gig was growing and I saw the potential for even more ventures for Detour Dave. I didn't have to look far for my next opportunity.

Both BAL and 98 ROCK were housed in the same building as WBAL-TV. As you approach Cold Spring Lane driving south on the Jones Falls Expressway, the main artery into Baltimore City, you can't miss the huge radio and TV towers that dominate the skyline from TV Hill. When WBAL-TV caught wind of how well-received the airborne traffic reports were, they wanted in. Their plan was to run a map of the Baltimore metro area with graphics highlighting the traffic congestion as I provided the voiceover from the plane. To capitalize on the Detour Dave brand, they created a caricature of my face atop of a plane and flew it into the picture when I was reporting from what they called "WBAL Flight 11."

With the TV station on board, the whole building was using my services. The money was getting better and better. My fan base was flourishing. Needless to say, I was ecstatic about the Detour Dave enterprise and how far it had come. It felt like we were just getting started, and I was excited to see where it would take me next.

ACOMPLISHMENTS

8. BUYING A PLANE

As opportunities for Detour Dave grew, I was open to expanding the business in unexpected directions. Buying a plane definitely fell into the "unexpected" category, but I'm a reasonable guy and am always willing to listen. Put an idea on my radar and I'll give it full consideration. During one of our daily, random conversations, my pilot, Mike, did just that.

As we cruised over the beltway, he asked me if I had ever thought about owning an airplane. I hadn't, but apparently he had, because he'd worked the numbers and thought there could be a decent profit in it. My first thought: "How on earth can I afford to buy an airplane?" My second: "Jody will think I've lost my mind if I tell her I want to buy an airplane." I had no idea what a small plane cost, but I assumed it was several hundred thousand dollars. Even if it were affordable, WBAL was renting a plane for our airborne reports, and I had no idea if they could get out of the contract. I had some homework to do.

Mike showed me that an airplane comparable to the rental, and all the necessary equipment, would cost $30,000 - $50,000 dollars. It was a lot of money, but with one zero less than I'd imagined. We calculated the insurance, gasoline, hangar storage, maintenance, and his pilot fee to determine the overhead. We knew that figure had to be in line with what BAL's vendor was charging for the station to consider switching. The biggest potential obstacle was my coming up with a 20% down payment. I was looking at $6,000 - $10,000, money I did not have. I decided to see if the idea would fly at BAL first and worry about the money later.

I talked with Jody at length and showed her what Mike and I had come up with. As always, she encouraged me to go for it. She believed in me and saw the potential to take Detour Dave in a new, lucrative direction. One hurdle down, two more to go.

Even with her blessing, I had lingering concerns. What if WBAL refused, or couldn't get out of the lease? Was I putting more financial pressure on my family than I should? Still, the more I thought about the benefits, the more sense it made. Traffic and weather together ... why not plane and reporter together in one complete package?

I should mention that because of my split shift, the stations did not consider me an employee. Even though I worked exclusively for them and had built my on-air identity as part of the BAL-98 Rock team, I was an independent contractor. My status had advantages and drawbacks. On the plus side there was no inherent conflict to my providing every aspect of the traffic service. A vendor is a vendor. On the negative side, I received no benefits. Health insurance, which would become so critical to me later, was completely my responsibility, as was saving for retirement. But every situation has its pros and cons— you take the good with the bad and make it work.

Instead of speculating about what they might say, I approached WBAL management to gauge their interest. They were very interested. They believed that working with a single trusted vendor like me was a win-win. My price was competitive, and their current plane rental agreement could end at any time. I was cleared for takeoff. Two hurdles down.

Now, the hard part: finding a plane and paying for it. Through my connections at Martin State Airport I asked an airplane broker to locate a Cessna 172. He found several; the one Mike and I liked cost $35,000, so I needed to scrape together a $7,000 down payment. As a young guy trying to build my own business, I didn't have that kind of money sitting in a bank account. I knew someone who did – my Uncle Morris, a successful businessman who had lived in Beverly Hills for 30 years. He was one of my biggest fans, but asking him—or anyone—for money was uncomfortable for me.

I stressed for a few days about phoning him, but knew that I had to ask or bail out of the deal. Everything was riding on Uncle Morris, so I crossed my fingers and called. I explained the idea, we talked some numbers, and without hesitation, he asked me where to send the check. That was even easier than the conversation with WBAL. Three hurdles down, all systems go. I hung up and thought, "Congrats, Detour. You're about to buy an airplane."

Once the deal was done and the glossy red and white, high-wing Cessna delivered, I decided to move the operation to the Carroll County Airport in Westminster, MD. It was closer to my house, and believe me, every minute counts when you drive to and from work twice a day, five days a week. The airport had no tower or air traffic controllers so we could take off and land at will. It's unthinkable with large commercial/passenger planes, but it was a huge timesaver for us. Fuel was less expensive there, and every discount helped the bottom line. As a bonus, the airport offered me an office from which I could deliver reports when weather was bad. Mike and I set up a desk, a microphone, and a phone line. We, and the business, took off.

In a matter of weeks I went from flying in someone else's plane to being the owner/operator of Detour Dave, Inc. I never imagined that traffic reporting could lead to a thriving business. I am forever grateful to Jody for believing in me, to my Uncle Morris for having sufficient faith in me and my vision to lend me the down payment, and to Mike for helping me to soar even higher. Without their support, Detour Dave, Inc. never would have happened.

As I look back on the birth of my company, so many lessons

emerge: thinking big, doing your due diligence, taking calculated risks, asking for help when you need it, and not being afraid of rejection. That's chapter one in the entrepreneur's playbook, and though I never considered myself as such, that's what I became. I worked hard, cultivated relationships, was discreet, and never burned a bridge. I sopped up advice like a sponge when more experienced colleagues were kind enough to offer it. I ignored nastiness and refused to play in that arena. I kept a positive attitude in spite of my doubts and always believed that if one venture didn't work out, the next one would.

In saying all that, I acknowledge fully that I was one lucky SOB in my professional life. I had one amazing career break after another and was fortunate enough to have the talent to sustain them. Choices I made for one reason – like moving back to Baltimore to marry Jody – always seemed to pay off with unforeseen benefits. My timing was impeccable. Friends, relatives and associates offered advisory and financial assistance when I needed it. Someone else's brilliant and generous insight catapulted me to new heights, whether it was Chris Emry's clever nickname or Mike's crazy idea to buy a plane. Believe me when I say that I take none of it for granted and count my many blessings every single day.

Still, when you are riding high, it's hard to fathom that everything you worked for can come crashing down in a split second. There is a painful truth in the cliché that what goes up must come down. It wasn't my plane, but my health, that took a nosedive. The biggest detour of my life was on the horizon, about to come into painful view.

I've often wondered if shooting down that turkey balloon had something to do with it. Nah, just kidding.

RESOURCEFULNESS

9. SHORTCUTS? NOT ALWAYS THE BEST COURSE.

Spending more than five hours a day, five days a week, in a small airplane has its ups and downs, literally. Soaring over the best view of just about everything in the Baltimore metro area is definitely one of the ups. Many others thought so as well, and our position in the skies quickly led to the creation of yet another business for Detour Dave, Inc.

About six months after I began doing my airborne traffic reports, individuals and companies started contacting me about snapping photos of their houses and businesses for personal and marketing purposes. "I'm up here anyway," I thought. "Why not shoot some pictures? Maybe I can even make a few bucks for my trouble. It will help pay for the plane."

Pilot Mike had moved on to a new opportunity by this time. My new pilot, Chip, had a quality camera, and was generous enough to let me use it when inquiries came in. We came up with a compensation arrangement and we were off. Believe me, I'm no professional photographer, but just about anyone with a decent camera and our vantage point could take excellent pictures.

Here was yet another unexpected opportunity falling out of the sky and into my lap. Was I born lucky or always in the right place at the right time? Whatever the case, I could now add aerial photography to the growing list of Detour Dave, Inc. businesses. I posted several shots of Oriole Park and Ravens Stadium to my website, Detourdave. com, to showcase the quality of my work. I included photos of sprawling mansions in the city and county for homeowners, as well as views of shopping centers, thinking that commercial real estate companies might take note. They did, and the requests for beauty shots of available properties started pouring in.

Chip and I captured most of the shots easily as we made our regular loop around the Baltimore beltway during traffic reports; we took other photos before or after my shift or on the weekends. Some pictures took perfect timing and tremendous piloting skill. For example, there are a number of office complexes near BWI-Marshall Airport, a major hub that serves the Baltimore-Washington area. Commercial real estate brokers would ask for a specific angle on a particular building, like from the end of a runway – nothing point-and-shoot about those photos! Chip would get a 30-second clearance from the tower to move into position while I snapped the picture. There were a few times when an incoming 747 or ascending Lear Jet would suddenly thunder into view, dwarfing the little Cessna and scaring us out of our seatbelts. We were like a hummingbird trying to compete with a condor for airspace. The condor always wins, so we retreated.

Thinking back on some of those split-second swerves it amazes me that we avoided an accident. I'm proud to say that in 20-plus years, with more than 15,000 hours of flight time, I've never been involved in a serious incident. I attribute that perfect record to the skill of my many pilots and their insistence that the plane be in peak condition before every flight. We entrusted the Cessna only to the best mechanics. We ran the pre-flight checklist every day, twice a day, no matter what. Safety was always our primary concern, and we never left it to chance. I think the pilots' motto says it best: I'd rather be on the ground wishing I were in the air than in the air wishing I were on the ground.

I've made my career helping people navigate jams and find short-cuts between points A and B. During that time, I've observed that taking shortcuts works in traffic, but not in life and business. Many of us attribute success to luck or timing. I prefer to chalk it up to taking all the necessary steps to do the job right. Cutting corners will catch up to you eventually. While doing so is rarely a matter of life and death, as it is in a small airplane, you can destroy trust and credibility it took you years to build in an instant. Being careless can end relationships or cause you to lose a job. Is skipping steps worth it when so much is at stake? My experience in the plane taught me that it's always worth the extra time and effort to check and double-check your work.

The next time you think about slacking, about doing just enough to slide by, think twice. Adapt the pilots' motto to your life: take the time to do it right, because you never save time doing it wrong.

FAMILIARITY

10. HOW TO LOSE A RIVER IN TEN MINUTES

Losing a river isn't easy, but on my first solo flight to qualify for my pilot's license, I lost it – in more ways than one.

The Susquehanna, the 464-mile long river that runs from upstate New York through Pennsylvania and into Maryland's Chesapeake Bay, is the largest river on the east coast that empties into the Atlantic Ocean. This is no little stream, but a major landmark that's impossible to miss from the air. It was to guide me on my test route that day. And I couldn't find it.

It wasn't as if this was the first time I'd covered this route. We – my many pilots and I – had flown over the river countless times during the 20 years I reported traffic from the air for two radio stations and one TV station. Getting from point A to point B by air should have been a snap. Still, just to be sure, I had carefully plotted my trip on a map earlier that morning with assistance from Chip, my pilot then and now. I was confident that I knew the course blind. And if I got lost, the mighty Susquehanna would keep me on course.

Once I was up in the air, alone in the cockpit, everything looked and felt different. Nothing on the ground was where it was supposed to be. Maybe it was because the wind was whipping at about 20 knots. Maybe I was used to having a pilot at the controls and hadn't fully adjusted to being solely responsible for what happened at 1,500 feet up.

Whatever the reason, I lost all perspective. I was struggling to recall what each instrument did. I scanned the horizon, twisted 360° in my seat, but no Susquehanna. I made a few loops of the area, trying to reassure myself that I wasn't lost. As the minutes crept by I could feel that telltale rush of adrenaline surge in the pit of my stomach. My anxiety was heading towards overload. I was in danger of losing control of my emotions, and even worse, of the plane.

After what felt like hours of mindless circling, I thought I spotted the river. I nudged the plane in that direction, only to find that the Tydings Bridge, which was supposed to cross it, wasn't there. I had no idea what body of water lay below me and no idea how to get back on course. That's when full-blown panic took over.

The discomfort was palpable. I felt warm, my face flushed. My breathing became more rapid and shallow. Sweat covered my forehead and brow. My heart was beating hard and fast. I felt dizzy, and dropped my hands from the wheel for who knows how long. I was a hapless soul bracing for the inevitable plummet to the ground.

When you're in a panic, time has no meaning. I must have sat stunned for just a few seconds or the plane would have gone into a deep dive. Something, and I can't tell you precisely what, triggered my internal guidance system just in time. I snapped to and saw that I was still aloft. My "muscle memory," that ability to call up and rely on experience without having to think, ordered me to look for something, anything, familiar.

I might as well have been on the moon—the landscape was that foreign to me. Since I didn't see anything to guide me, I knew I had to rely on something else to get me safely back to the ground. Because the plane was used for real-time traffic reporting, the two-way radio was tied directly to one WBAL radio. I grabbed the handset and squeaked out a tentative, "Hi?" praying that someone would acknowledge me. No response.

I tried again, this time a little stronger. "Can anyone hear me? Hello?" Within 10 seconds I heard a voice on the other end. "Dave, what's up?" It was enough to calm my shaking hands and refocus my attention. I wasn't alone. Maybe now I had a real chance to make it home safely.

After all that sweat and anguish, and with miles to go before I landed, did I ask for help or admit that I was lost? I'm a man, so I'll give you one guess. How would it look for the "eye in the sky" to flop on his first solo run? To reveal an imagined weakness? (I would learn soon enough that relying on others when you need support is nothing to be ashamed of).

Instead, I mustered the best approximation of my radio voice and did what came naturally from the cockpit: I pretended to deliver a traffic report. I said, "Hey, I'm soloing today and want to see if I can talk and fly at the same time. Got 15 seconds to tell me how I sound?" He said, "Sure," and I started talking.

Somehow, that familiar rhythm, those comfortable terms, cleared my head and revived my confidence. As I ran through my daily vocabulary, I started to recognize some landmarks below. There, finally, was the Susquehanna, exactly where it was supposed to be. I grabbed the wheel with new-found authority and righted my course. I don't recall thanking my colleague for picking up the radio that day, so I'd like to do so now. It was a routine response to him; it was a lifesaver for me.

As I banked the plane toward Westminster, I pointed to the sky above and thanked God for giving me the strength to overcome that unnerving and potentially life-threatening incident. I remember vowing to myself, "If I get back alive, I'm never going solo again!"

After much internal debate, I kept that pact—not out of fear, but from a deeper respect for the risk versus the reward of flying alone. No matter how diligently I prepared, the unexpected could happen in a split second: a sudden burst of weather, a mechanical failure, or the onset of illness presented huge risks that a co-pilot could mitigate. I was a father, husband, son, and bread winner. There was no shame in flying with a buddy. On the contrary, it felt like the wise and responsible thing to do.

In virtually every aspect of our lives, there are times when going it alone makes sense; other times, working with a partner or team delivers better results. Deciding how you'll travel starts with weighing all the factors you know and developing a clear flight plan for the situation. Use the risk/reward calculation and take it from there. Be flexible enough to pivot when something isn't working as expected. You can blindly circle on a losing course, or you can redirect your energies to a strategy that will pay off.

When all else fails, trust your instincts. That impromptu traffic report was my inner auto-pilot helping me overcome the panic, reorient myself, and execute a soft landing. I believe that we all have the inner resources to prevail over the toughest of times; often it takes being in the moment to make us realize just how resourceful we are.

As for the Susquehanna, it's still one of the most beautiful rivers in America from any vantage point. Finding it helped me find my courage.

GROUNDED

11. CHANGING GEARS

The airspace between Baltimore and Washington is the most restricted in the world. The sheer number of strategic targets—the White House, the Pentagon, the Capitol, Andrews Air Force Base and Camp David—is staggering. Pilots must file specific flight plans every time they take off anywhere in the region. Since we went up twice a day five days a week, the air traffic controllers allowed us to register and use our tail number as our identifier instead of submitting 10 identical flight plans each week.

When I started airborne reports in the rental plane, we used Martin State Airport in eastern Baltimore County. It was a busy regional airport, serving private, commercial and Air National Guard craft as well as multiple traffic planes and one helicopter. All of the traffic reporters were assigned a specific altitude at which to fly; since we were the first to register our plane we had our choice of airspace. We selected 1400 feet, the lowest altitude, so we could be as close as possible to the action and see maximum detail. Planes flying for rival radio/TV stations were given altitudes of 1600, 1800 and 2000 feet. I know a separation of only 200 feet sounds dangerously close, but the pilots were in constant communication and aware of each other's whereabouts at all times.

We also had the advantage of keeping the Cessna in a warm, commercial hangar while many of the other reporters tethered their planes outside, regardless of the weather. I pitied the poor pilots, scraping ice and snow off the planes on frigid winter mornings, while we pulled our plane from its toasty hangar and took off. Thank you, BAL!

Broadcasting from the plane was fun and carefree compared to the commuters inching their way around the beltway in the daily struggle to get to work on time. There we were, soaring overhead, with only the birds for company. On a clear day we could see as far as the Bay Bridge or the Washington Monument, both of which were more than 50 miles away. It was a gorgeous view and a phenomenal job, and I felt like the luckiest guy in the troposphere.

People often ask me how my live reports from the plane made it to their radios. We used a broadcast-quality two-way radio that sent my voice to the large WBAL-TV antenna rising from TV Hill. The signal then went through the radio stations' control board and out to the listening public. The entire process only took a few seconds, so there was no discernible delay between my voice and the listeners' ears. The closer to the antenna, the better the sound quality; we tried to stay within a 50-mile radius of the station.

In early 2001, WBAL-TV installed high-definition (HD) equipment onto the antenna tower. The new technology made their signal stronger and on-screen images significantly brighter and sharper. It was a brilliant innovation for the TV station, but when we flew over certain areas the new equipment blocked our signal. We were clear as a bell one moment and broken up or barely audible the next. I could hear in my headset when my voice deteriorated into static-filled jibberish. The poor quality was frustrating, and we hated the limitations on our flying range. If we were restricted, our reports weren't the most comprehensive. If all our listeners heard was static, why listen?

For months we tried desperately to work through the issue. I remember giving hand signals to my pilot to move the plane left or right to keep the strong signal on the air. It was like the famous cell-phone commercial: "Can you hear me now?" We decided to ground the plane and report from the station until the engineers could resolve the problem.

We didn't have to wait long for a final resolution. On September 11, 2001, just after my last morning broadcast, a 767 airliner flew into one of New York's Twin Towers. Everyone assumed it was a freak accident until 18 minutes later, when a second 767 hit the South Tower near the 60th floor.

It was bedlam inside the WBAL building. Reporters scrambled for information; even the network and cable news outlets were struggling to make sense of the mind-boggling events. We went "wall-to-wall" with coverage for the next several hours because accurate information was slow to emerge. The subsequent attack on the Pentagon and the crash in Shanksville, PA, only added to the confusion.

Over the next 24 hours, the nation came to understand that we had been hit by senseless acts of terror. We didn't fully grasp the many ways in which our daily lives would change, but it was clear that we would feel the after-effects of 9/11 for decades to come. One of the first and most obvious changes was in air traffic. The days of running through airports at the last minute to catch a flight were over. As far as WBAL management was concerned, so were airborne traffic reports. The FAA had issued a moratorium on small plane traffic over Baltimore/Washington airspace, so we were shut down for the fore-seeable future. Even without the new restrictions, the risks far out-weighed the benefits. I applauded the decision. Frankly, I would have been uneasy flying given our proximity to the nation's capital.

Station management knew that ending the airborne reports didn't put an end to my many plane-related expenses. They gener-ously offered to continue paying me the rental for six months so I could cover the cost of the pilot, hangar, insurance and loan. I hadn't expected it, but was grateful that they had given me time to figure out what to do with my now-useless bird.

While 9/11 was the tragic catalyst for our grounding, technology eventually would have had the same effect. Traffic cameras were being erected around the beltway, I-95 and other major arteries, giving us access to hundreds of locations via the computer. Loyal "traffic trouble" callers reported like clockwork the backups and accidents they encountered on their daily commutes. Police scanners and a roster of agencies fed us information. The hardware, software, infrastructure, and old-fashioned eyes on the ground made our twice-daily ascent obsolete. And while I had originally hated the HD system for interfering with our reports, it made us more reliable as we moved into this new era that changed everything.

LESSONS

12. NEVER BURN A BRIDGE

I have learned so much from so many wonderful people at different organizations; it's hard to distill a single life lesson. Let me share two that I've found invaluable. The first is to take measured risks and treat failure as an opportunity. I call it "fearless flexibility." The second, closely tied to those inevitable disappointments, is one I can't say often enough: never, ever burn bridges.

Fearless flexibility covers a lot of ground, so let me provide some examples.

When I walked into my first radio audition at the University of Maryland, I knew that there was more at stake for me than getting a part-time gig at a tiny station. If I couldn't cut it, I would have to completely re-think my future. I could have let the fear of failure derail me, but I went in with a positive attitude and gave it my all. The thought that it might not pan out was always in the back of my mind, but I locked it there and didn't let the "what if" affect my performance. I focused on the task at hand so I could do my best. If it wasn't good enough, I trusted that I'd come up with a new plan.

Then there's Jody, my wife and partner through all the ups and downs for, as of this writing, almost 30 years. Pursuing her was absolutely the right and best decision for me. But giving up my first on-air job in State College, PA to do so was a huge risk – what if the relationship had flamed out? What if I'd moved home and been unable to find a job? I've learned that it's not the presence of the risk, but how I react to it, that makes all the difference. I banished the "what if" thinking that could have paralyzed me. I trusted my gut that making the choice to move home would work out on all fronts—and it has, even with all the detours, roadblocks and sinkholes on the road we've traveled together.

My dismissal from the Bel Air station, an unforeseen detour to be sure, was an experience that illustrates both lessons beautifully. Getting fired is not on anyone's bucket list, especially when we think we're bringing our A-game every day. Sometimes, though, having change forced on you can be a gift. All of us get settled in a job or a relationship and coast on the inertia. We settle instead of reaching for the next goal. Losing my job helped me find my professional future. It pushed me to try something I had never considered. I was open to it; I set my fears aside, and it became my life's work. It was the best thing that could have happened to me.

Of course, in the moment, it's hard to keep your composure. Tempting as it is to spout off, no matter what the circumstance, you must leave a situation as gracefully as you entered it. Getting angry, bad-mouthing others—that's for the playground, not the workplace. Besides being in extremely bad form, it reflects poorly on you and can come back to haunt you in the long run. I cannot tell you how often I've reached out to or been approached by a connection that didn't work out as intended; in almost every instance, there's been a cordial and sincere desire to help on both ends, because we kept it civil. Let the bridge stand and keep the matches in your pocket.

In all those early years I worked hard to be liked in a professional manner. I don't mean kissing up—I mean being genuine, open and accepting the wisdom others were willing to share, eagerly completing tasks that may have been beneath my skill set simply because it was important to be a team player. I tolerated others' quirks without judging. None of those traits are easy, but they are all essential.

Life is inherently filled with risk. Trust yourself to make the wisest choice at the moment based on what you know and what you believe. I'm not advocating a coin flip; pay attention to the facts on the ground and your gut feeling. Ask a trusted advisor for an opinion. Then dive in fearlessly with the understanding that what you decide today may take a U-turn tomorrow. Keeping those bridges intact can save you a lot of drive time the next time you find yourself moving in a new direction.

SECTION 2 ➤

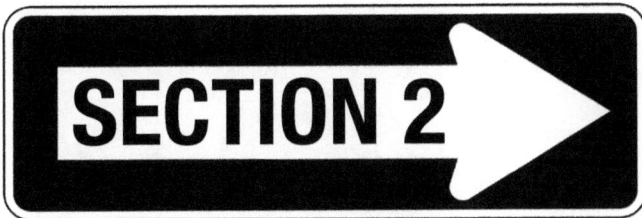

MY HEALTH HITS A ROADBLOCK

CANCER

13. DANGEROUS TERRITORY

I was in the first semester of my junior year at the University of Maryland, rooming with my buddy Troy and thoroughly enjoying every aspect of college life. Never much of a partier or early riser, I did love playing late-night card games with the guys on our floor. I scheduled my classes after 10 a.m. so I could sleep in. Most of my courses were now in my Radio/TV major, so the work was in my sweet spot. I was learning so much and getting hands-on experience in the campus studios. I was dating a great girl named Sheryl, playing pick-up basketball, working out, going to Terps games, and taking part in all the activities College Park had to offer. Socially and academically, everything was exactly as I'd hoped it would be.

Then, around Thanksgiving, I began having trouble sleeping through the night. I'd wake up suddenly with a pain in my chest. It wasn't the kind of pain you'd have with a heart issue; it was more of a constant throbbing, like the pounding sensation you feel with a headache, but below my neck and in the middle of my sternum. I thought I might have strained my chest playing basketball, or pulled a muscle lifting weights. I'd had many minor muscle injuries over the years playing sports, so I did what most people do: I ignored it and hoped it would pass.

I didn't notice it during the day when I was busy. But when I lay down at night, especially when the floor was quiet, I felt it acutely. After a few weeks of waking up in pain, I told Troy. He was adamant that I go home and see my doctor. I called my mom, who quickly made an appointment.

As I lay on the exam table, we could see a small lump protruding from my chest. The doctor examined it but couldn't make a precise diagnosis. He didn't seem especially worried about it, but my mom wasn't satisfied. She wanted to know exactly what it was and insisted that I see another doctor. She had had thyroid cancer and wasn't taking any chances.

She made an appointment with Dr. Elmer Hoffman, a general surgeon whom she knew and trusted. He examined me and recommended performing a biopsy on the lump. He said, "It could be a number of things, but I don't want to jump to any conclusions. A biopsy will tell us for sure what's going on. We can do it here in my office, send out the sample, and we'll know something definitive in a few days."

A few days? Back then that sounded like a lifetime to me. I was at a critical juncture in my education. I didn't want to miss classes or all the fun I was having. I asked him for some odds on what it might be. He responded that it could be something as benign as a swollen lymph node or something much more serious. He didn't utter the word "cancer" that I recall, so that possibility never entered my mind. I was thinking that, at worst, I'd suffered a huge inconvenience that might set me back a few weeks. I was annoyed that I might have to cram to catch up, or miss an upcoming football game. Pretty naïve, but what would you expect from a healthy 20-year-old?

After Dr. Hoffman took the biopsy, I returned to College Park and waited. I had hoped that being at school would distract me, but until the pathology report came back I felt helpless, anxious, and unable to concentrate on much else. One week later I returned to his office for the results. Dr. Hoffman got right to the point: "Dave, the test results show that you have Hodgkin's lymphoma, a type of cancer that affects the immune system. Cancerous cells are growing unchecked outside your lymphatic system. You will need treatment, and I'm making you an appointment now with a colleague who is an oncologist, a cancer specialist. You'll be in good hands."

He kept talking but all I heard was "cancer." *Cancer? At 20? How could this be?* I don't remember crying, but I do remember feeling like I'd been hit by a giant wave and struggling to catch my breath. There were so many questions running through my mind. *Is college over for me? Can we fight it?* And of course, the big one: *am I dying?* Dr. Hoffman told me that the specialist, Dr. Leonard Lichtenfeld, would see me that day to walk me through the next steps. "He's a great doctor and a good man. I'm sure he will be able to answer all of your questions in far greater detail."

Dr. Lichtenfeld's office was around the corner in the same building. I was relieved that he could see me; if I'd had to wait one more day to know what lay ahead, I'm not sure I could have handled it. I was terrified, but needed answers to the big life related questions I'd posed to Dr. Hoffman. As we sat in the waiting room my legs were shaking. When his nurse called me back to his office, I wasn't sure I could walk. My mom discreetly put her hand on my back and gently guided me down the hall.

He shook my hand and insisted that I call him "Dr. Len." His soothing manner put me at ease immediately. I needed to hear what he had to say, and the first words out of his mouth were magic: "Dave, this type of cancer is highly treatable, so don't panic." That was enough to calm my churning stomach and racing mind. *OK, I'm not dying. That's better than good. Now what do we do?*

He told me that I would have to undergo more tests to understand what stage the cancer was in – had it spread outside of the lymph nodes and, if so, how extensively – so he could devise a treatment plan to eradicate it. He repeated that, of all the cancers I could have, Hodgkin's was one of the better ones. *A good cancer?* I couldn't imagine such a thing, but as I've learned, all cancers are not created equal.

He explained more about the lymphatic system so I would understand what was going on inside my body. Lymph nodes are filter-like structures that help carry harmful viruses and bacteria out of the body. The spleen, tonsils and thymus are major lymph nodes/organs; 600-700 smaller nodes are spread throughout the body. You've probably felt the ones under your jaw when you've had a bad cold and thought, "I have swollen glands." A network of vessels carries clear lymph fluid containing white blood cells to the nodes to fight infection. Typically, the nodes are small and hard to detect, but when there is an infection the nodes swell. Once the infection clears, the nodes return to normal size. Not so with cancer, which is why the node in my chest was so prominent.

If you were diagnosed today with Hodgkin's, you'd be whisked into a tunnel for an MRI or PET scan. In 1982, advanced imaging technologies didn't exist. To see whether cancerous cells were in any other lymph glands a surgeon would perform a "staging laparotomy," which would cut me open from neck to groin. The surgeon would biopsy as many lymph nodes as he thought necessary, and Dr. Len would base my treatment on the results.

I wasn't thrilled at the prospect of being sawed in half, but what choice did I have? Dr. Len scheduled the operation after the semester ended so I could return to College Park and complete my classes. That convinced me that I wasn't dying – I figured he'd rush me into surgery if I was on my way out. It also allowed me to return to my routine, which I craved. I knew that card games, the Terps, and my buddies would be the best medicine for me in the short term.

SURGERY

14. WAITING FOR WORD

It took extra effort to keep my studies and my mental health on track during the remainder of the semester. Concentrating was difficult – the impending surgery intruded constantly. It was the classic mind game of "don't think about the pink elephant." Still, I was determined to survive finals week and pass all my exams. I wasn't sure how long I'd be out for treatment, so it was important to earn as many credits as I could. As I closed the last blue book, I knew that the biggest test of my young life was just ahead. While my classmates were packing up for a relaxing winter break, I was on my way to Baltimore to meet Dr. Juan Juantegy, the highly regarded thoracic surgeon who would perform my laparotomy.

The way Dr. Len had explained it, Dr. Juantegy had to take small amounts of tissue from all the major lymph nodes in my body and examine them for abnormal cell growth. He would sample the lymph nodes in my armpits, chest, neck, groin and spleen. He told me to expect my spleen to be removed, dissected, and examined for tumors as a precaution. I wasn't exactly sure what a spleen did, but he assured me that I could live a perfectly normal life without one.

A few days before the procedure, I met with Dr. Juantegy for a more detailed description of what to expect. He knew that I played soccer, and he had played on a national team, so we bonded quickly over our mutual love of the sport. He was a personable guy, but direct. He explained that he would cut an opening from my chest to my navel and start collecting tissue. He cautioned me that this was a major operation, with weeks of painful recuperation and severely limited movement. I'd be in the hospital for at least a week. As I rose to leave his office, he promised that I would live a long and happy life, cancer free. I told him that I'd hold him to it.

I appreciated his candor and reassurance, but his description of the operation left me a bit queasy. I was 20 and had been in perfect health until then. I'd never been to the hospital for anything, so the whole experience was overwhelming. The operation and painful recovery were just the first part of it. The treatment to eradicate the cancer would not be pleasant. And if the cancer had spread, I'd have to undergo more drastic treatment. Any way you sliced me, the prospects for the next few months were grim.

Instead of dwelling on the "what-ifs", I decided to approach each phase of treatment individually, one step at a time. It was just too big a mountain to climb in one ascent. I kept thinking, "Just get through this. I'll deal with that later." It was a survival mechanism that served me well through the ensuing months, and again 28 years later.

The surgery was scheduled for a few days after our meeting. I checked in to Sinai Hospital and was immediately put into a room and handed a thin hospital gown. I was cold and anxious, but my mom, step-dad and girlfriend Sheryl kept my spirits up. I signed the consent forms, kissed everyone, and, in a matter of minutes, the nurses wheeled me to the OR. I remember shaking almost uncontrollably as the gurney rolled closer to the OR, from nerves and the cold. One of the nurses gave me a heated blanket and asked if I wanted something to calm me down. "Yes!" I said before she could finish her sentence.

The operating room was colder than the hallway, both in

temperature and appearance. The overhead lights were blindingly bright, and everything in the room was either stark white or stainless steel – sterile and unwelcoming. I heard music in the background; I would have preferred the Oriole's game to distract me but it was the off season. I lay there freezing, waiting for something to happen, as nurses and doctors bustled in and out. I could hear them speaking in hushed tones as they placed surgical instruments on the trays and adjusted the harsh lights. I felt like a prisoner awaiting his execution. But to keep my stomach empty for the anesthesia, I hadn't eaten a last meal—yet another indignity.

Just as I was about to run screaming from the OR, the sedative kicked in, and I felt my body start to relax as I grew drowsy. I was lifted from the gurney onto the operating table, which was much smaller and less comfortable. As I squirmed, Dr. Juantegy entered the OR in full surgical gear. He took my hand and reassured me that everything was going to be OK. The anesthesiologist was in position behind my head, and the nurse leaned in. "We're going to put some sleepy juice into your IV now. Just relax and let it do its job." The music faded, and I was out.

I woke up in the recovery room struggling to regain my wits. Nurses were asking if I could hear them. I nodded yes, but was too groggy to speak. My entire body was wrapped in mummy-like bandages so tight I could barely move, but I felt no pain. My throat was sore from the breathing tube, which I suppose they inserted once I was under. I nodded in and out for the next hour or so as the nurses continued to check my vitals.

My mom came in first, then my stepdad and Sheryl. My mom told me that Dr. Juantegy was pleased with how the operation had gone. He was able to collect all the necessary tissue samples and had removed my spleen. I continued to drift in and out for the next few hours. That "sleepy juice" was powerful stuff, and it took most of the day for me to wake up fully.

I'd be in the hospital the entire week, so the nurses could monitor my stem-to-stern incision and the stitches that held it together. If I moved too much, there was a danger that it could pop open, a disgusting prospect that I dealt with years later under even more dire circumstances. The pain was rough the first two days, but medication made it bearable. Believe it or not, my biggest issue was lying still. I was always in motion with sports and activities, so locking myself into one position was difficult and extremely dull.

Pathology needed a week to review all the tissue samples and determine whether the cancer had spread beyond my sternum, the site of the tumor. Of course, I worried about those pathology reports no matter how I tried to distract myself. *Was the cancer confined to my chest, or had it metastisized? Would I, as Dr. Juantegy promised, live a long healthy life, or would they find cancer in all my lymph nodes? Was more surgery in my future? Chemo?*

I had no choice but to stay still and wait for the results. One step at a time. One step at a time.

SOLUTION

15. THE CURE BECOMES A CURSE

After sitting perfectly still for a week, with only my mind spinning, the pathology report was complete. Dr. Lichtenfeld came into my hospital room and delivered the terrific news: the Hodgkin's had not spread. The lymph nodes and spleen were clear. Since the cancer was confined to the chest, he would treat it and my abdomen with radiation therapy. Chemotherapy would needlessly kill good cells all over my body and make me feel nauseated, so that was not part of the plan. "Dave," he said, "this cancer is very treatable. We caught it early. You're going to do well with the radiation and be cured. You can relax now. The worst is over."

I was thrilled. The treatment didn't sound too bad, and he was sure he could eliminate the cancer. This was everything I had hoped for. For the first time in weeks, I could breathe.

After I was discharged from the hospital and mobile again, my mom and I met with Dr. Lichtenfeld to review the treatment plan in depth. I would receive radiation to my chest four days a week for four weeks. After that round was complete, as a precaution, I'd receive another four weeks of radiation to my abdomen.

He introduced me to Dr. Gunam Emmanuel, the radiation oncologist who would be handling my case. When I first met him I had some difficulty understanding him. He was originally from India and had a thick accent. Clear communication was essential to me, and I was concerned about whether he was the right doctor for me. Yet after our initial visit, I realized there was something special about him. I'm not sure if it was his smile, body language, or demeanor, but we connected on a deep level. He was straightforward yet compassionate. He said we would kick the cancer and make me well. That was the clear communication I needed to hear. And I liked that he used the pronoun "we." This was a team effort – he was with me every step of the way.

Even though he and Dr. Lichtenfeld had tried to prepare me for the radiation therapy, walking into the treatment room for my first round was terrifying. It was cold and dark with a large, UFO-like metal object hanging from the ceiling. In the center of the room was a slim table similar to the one in the OR. That was it. One of the radiation techs instructed me to lie on the table. She put foam blocks around my neck and a lead apron over my lap to prevent radiation from hitting any other areas. Unbeknownst to me at the time, radiation can negatively affect fertility; Jody and I discovered that fact when we were trying to start a family. Despite the lead apron, the radiation had reduced my sperm count significantly, and it took some time before Alix was on the way. We overcame that side effect again four years later with Brooks.

As I lay there waiting for the first beam to zap me, I started shaking. The combination of high anxiety and low temperature was too much. The treatment room was eerie, like something out of a bad sci-fi movie – and I was the object of the alien experiment. I had no idea what the radiation would feel like, but I wasn't in the mood for more pain. The tech came over and asked if I was OK. I confessed that I was scared, and she reassured me that I wouldn't feel a thing. I took a deep breath and said, "Let's do this!"

The tech went into a small anteroom and turned off the lights. I was on the table in complete, chilling blackness, waiting for the radiation to begin. When she flipped the switch, the UFO aimed a blinding beam directly at my chest and emitted a high-pitched shriek that reminded me of "The Twilight Zone." Since there was nothing on the walls to absorb noise, the screeching echoed throughout the room and through my body. It was one of the most grating sounds I'd ever heard, but I had to lie there and endure it. True, I didn't feel anything, but between the noise and the brightness it was all I could do to keep from jumping off the table and fleeing. I kept saying to myself, "Do not flip out. Do NOT flip out. This is the cure. This is the cure." The treatment lasted only 10 minutes. I thought the shrieking would never end. I hated it. But I had to embrace it if I wanted to live.

Following the first treatment, I confided to Dr. Emmanuel that I'd been on the verge of passing out from anxiety. He listened patiently to my concerns, but reiterated how much it was helping me. "I know it is uncomfortable, but try to imagine the beam killing the cancer cells. Other patients have told me that visualizing is helpful. I promise you that it will get easier over time." At my next appointment, I talked to a couple of veteran patients in the waiting room; all of them assured me that it became routine after a while, and that made me feel better as well. As the treatments progressed, the cold, noise, and darkness became easier to tolerate.

Once the four weeks were done, my doctors reported that the chest tumor was shrinking. They were pleased with my progress, and I was starting to believe that I would be cured. They gave me two weeks off to recover from the initial round, and then I was back on the table to have my abdomen zapped.

Because of the time I needed to complete my therapy, I had to take a medical leave of absence from College Park for the spring semester. My girlfriend Sheryl knew I was unhappy about falling behind, so she set me up to take courses through the cooperative extension service at Maryland. The courses aired on Maryland Public Television – online classes hadn't been invented in 1982. I watched and would take the finals when I returned to College Park. Another problem solved.

After my brief respite from the black room, I started my second round of radiation. It proved much more difficult to stomach, literally. The beam was aimed directly at my abdomen, and after the first few treatments I was overcome with stomach-churning nausea. My mom drove me to and from therapy, and by the time we pulled into the driveway after each session I'd be out of the car heaving on the grass. It was disgusting, but beyond my control. I kept telling myself *this isn't forever. Just a few more weeks to go.* My mom was a trooper. I'm sure she was appalled that I was throwing up in front of the neighbors, but she just let me be and got on with her day.

Once the abdominal series was done, I waited, hoping that the tumor was shrinking and the cancer cells eradicated. I was scheduled for a series of follow-up chest X-rays and CT scans; if there was no evidence of the tumor after a few months, I would be in remission. If I was cancer-free after five years, I was officially cured. All the initial tests looked great, so now it was up to me to keep my appointments, live my life and hope for the best.

Even with such an optimistic prognosis, the Hodgkin's ordeal had taken a physical and mental toll. Being opened from neck to navel followed by months of radiation had traumatized my body. Getting a cancer diagnosis at 20 and the ensuing uncertainty about my future left me emotionally depleted. I found myself weeping frequently, anxious and depressed. I consulted a therapist who helped me identify my fears and learn coping skills to deal with them. I remain a big believer in getting help when you need it – going it alone is rough and unproductive. Better to reach out than to suffer.

When my mother's brother, Uncle Morris, heard about my emotional state, he and his wife, Aunt Mickie, insisted that I fly to L.A. and spend several weeks with them in Beverly Hills. "We'll fatten you up. Come on out and lounge by the pool!" he said. They had a beautiful home and were ready to pamper me. How could I say no? I spent four weeks basking in the sunshine, seeing the sights and being catered to by my favorite aunt and uncle. It was a luxurious vacation that, along with the therapy, helped to restore my spirits. This wasn't the only time Uncle Morris came to my rescue. He played a vital role at all the important moments in my life. He's gone now, but will forever be in my heart.

Obviously the five-year mark came and went, and I remained cancer-free. Little did I know that the seeds of an even more devastating ordeal had been planted in my body. It took almost 30 years to emerge, but when it hit me heading home on that scorching Sunday morning, it was more powerful and more damaging than any laser beam.

TRUST

16. MY BIGGEST DETOUR: THE REST OF THE STORY

Dying the way I did, on the softball field 28 years after I was cured, is scary, but only in retrospect. I tumbled so suddenly that I didn't feel it. I lay there, cold and ashen along the dugout fence, but I have no memory of it. I suppose that if you have to die, that's the way to do it: boom and out. It's *after* you come back that the pain, in all its forms, kicks in. The emotional toll brought on by fear, the physical distress at every phase of treatment, the grueling recoveries. Don't get me wrong – you'll never hear me complaining. Living to tell my tale is a gift.

As I lay unconscious, Mike began chest compressions while Scott blew air into my lungs and monitored my pulse in a frantic effort to revive me. Someone called 911, someone else called Jody. Within 30 seconds, Scott detected a light pulse, and the color rushed back to my face as blood began to flow. As quickly as I'd died I was back. Remarkable.

As I came to I saw dozens of concerned faces hovering above me. I was dazed and disoriented, and tried to get up. Scott gently restrained me and told me to lie still and rest. He later shared that instead of asking what had happened to me, I asked, "Did I score? Did we win?"

Once a weekend warrior, always a weekend warrior, I guess. I could feel the pain in the front of my head where I'd hit the fence and saw that my uniform was caked with dirt. But I still had no idea how close I'd come to the end of my life. Wisely, no one volunteered any information. I was in shock, and no one wanted to upset me further.

I lay on the ground, my head throbbing, the sirens getting louder and louder as the ambulance approached the field. With everyone watching anxiously, the paramedics got to work. As soon as I was stable they loaded me onto the stretcher and rushed me to Northwest Hospital's ER for an evaluation. My then-16-year-old son, Brooks, who had come to watch me play, drove behind the ambulance; fortunately, one of my teammates had led him away from the scene just in case I hadn't regained consciousness.

At Northwest, the initial treatment focused on my head injury since I'd hit the ground pretty hard on my way down. A concussion was likely, but Scott suspected a serious cardiac issue and recommended to Jody that I be moved to the University of Maryland Medical Center (UMMC), one of the region's leading medical institutions. He told her that UMMC would be better equipped to diagnose and handle my care if his suspicions proved correct. Keep in mind that, at this point, neither of us knew Scott at all. I had barely met him, and Jody was worried sick seeing me on that exam table. The ER physician was kind and, I'm sure, capable, but he wasn't a cardiologist. We placed our trust in Scott, and it proved to be a life-saving decision.

I endured another agonizing ambulance ride to UMMC, still in pain and in the dark about my condition. I remember that there was no air conditioning, and it was a stifling 99 degrees outside; I can only imagine how hot it was in the vehicle. Who transports a cardiac patient in that kind of heat? It was a poor decision, but I was in no condition to argue. So I lay on the stretcher with gritted teeth and suffered, sweating all the way down the Jones Falls Expressway. If only that airless ride had been the worst of it. It would be a few days and a few dozen uncomfortable tests later before I understood how big a detour this was going to be.

At UMMC, Scott performed an echocardiogram, a sonogram that creates a dimensional picture of the heart, followed the next day by a cardiac catheterization. He threaded a thin, flexible tube through a major artery in my groin and into my heart. He then injected dye into the tube and took images of my heart to detect any abnormalities. The results were so unexpected that we could barely comprehend them: the four main arteries leading to my heart were more than 80% blocked. Scott told me that I needed quadruple bypass surgery NOW to correct the problem.

I had always thought of bypass surgery as a procedure for older men who were overweight and out of shape, who took statins for cholesterol and diuretics for high blood pressure. Yet here I was, a relatively young guy in my late 40's who exercised regularly, never smoked, and was a healthy weight. I had no family history of heart disease. I didn't take any medications. Jody and I were completely stunned by the diagnosis. Neither of us could fathom how this had happened; when Scott explained *why* it had happened, I thought back to the Hodgkin's disease I'd overcame decades earlier.

When I was diagnosed, the state of-the-art treatment was to blast the cancer with massive amounts of radiation. Oncologists knew that radiation was effective but they weren't sure how much was enough. To kill the abnormal cells, they went overboard. This cure proved a curse for me and many other Hodgkin's survivors. Scar tissue formed around my heart. Over the next 20+ years, my arteries narrowed until the blood flow was almost completely shut off. I had absolutely no clue because, until I collapsed, I'd had no noticeable symptoms of heart disease.

I remember lying in the hospital bed speechless with disbelief – and for a guy who made his living by talking, that was unusual. I was grateful to be alive, of course, but terrified of what it would take to fully recover from such a serious condition. Jody and I had virtually no time to digest how it might affect our future. Scott made it crystal clear that there was no time for delay. One incident could lead to another, and I might not be so lucky the next time. He arranged a meeting with a heart surgeon, Dr. Jamie Brown, and we scheduled the operation for his first available surgical slot on Wednesday.

After reviewing the details of the operation with Dr. Brown – and they were gruesome – I was surprised at how calm I felt. He was talking about cracking open my chest, taking arteries from other parts of my body, grafting them to my heart, and restarting the blood flow. But what could possibly be scarier than dying? True, I faced a long, complicated surgery, but I felt no anxiety.

Maybe it was because I'd prevailed over cancer. Maybe Scott's being on the ball field that day convinced me that I was given another chance for a reason. Maybe the wonderful medical team gave me confidence. Maybe it was just my competitive spirit saying, "Let's do this. Let's get on with it, the sooner the better." Whatever magic combination of factors gave me courage, I was at peace.

On Wednesday morning I was understandably nervous, not so much about going under the knife but about the long and arduous recovery that would follow. I kissed Jody, Brooks and Alix and felt so lucky to have them at my side. As the attendants wheeled me toward the OR I chanted, "Fix that HEART! Fix that HEART!" And I believed they would.

Seven hours later, the first major detour on my long road to recovery was over. Dr. Brown had taken two healthy arteries from my arms, one from a leg and one from my chest, and grafted them onto my now-useless heart arteries. He successfully connected them to my heart, and blood was flowing freely. The relief was overwhelming for me and my family. One hurdle down, a hundred more to go. The first one popped up just 10 days later.

My doctors tracked my progress for a week or so before deciding on their next steps. They wanted to make sure that there were no complications from the bypass and that blood was circulating as it should. While all systems were "Go" on that front, they remained concerned about the possibility of another sudden cardiac arrest – and that I wouldn't be as lucky the next time.

To guard against that possibility, the doctors decided to insert a defibrillator, a small, battery-powered device that shocks the heart back into rhythm if it stops. About the size of a half-dollar, the defibrillator is placed under the skin just below the collarbone and attached to the heart with tiny wires. Mine was inserted 10 days after the bypass with no ill effects, other than that it protrudes about ½ inch and is clearly visible under my skin. Typically, I keep my shirt on in public, so no big deal. In fact, I like knowing that it's there. It provides extra protection, and it doesn't interfere with my day-to-day activities. Occasionally I'll reach over and give it a little tap of thanks. I hope I never need it, but it's there for me if I do.

It would be impossible to go through an experience like this without learning some powerful lessons. The first is gratitude, which covers so many bases in my story. I'm grateful that, for whatever reason, Scott and Mike were on the field that day. They have become my close friends for life. I'm grateful for my supportive family, who struggled along with me on my challenging journey back to health. I owe a huge debt to the amazing medical professionals who took such great care of me. I'm grateful for the friends and extended family who sat with Jody at the hospital, made meals, called daily, ran errands, and did what they could to make her life easier. I'm incredibly thankful that WBAL gave me time to heal and showed such generosity. I'm grateful to our listeners for their thousands of emails, posts, cards and letters.

I mentioned trust earlier, and I want to emphasize how important it is in all phases of your life. There are times when you must recognize that others know more than you do and let them take over. It's amazing how, when you let someone else take the wheel, you see for the first time all the things you missed while you were struggling to maintain control. Letting go is eye-opening in every sense of the word.

The year I spent recovering taught me the beauty of patience. I lost my life, albeit only for an instant, but there was no easy way back from that moment. I lost ground as often as I gained it. I had to accept my limitations and live in the moment. Going from 60 mph to 10 is frustrating, but I focus on what I CAN do, not what I can't. I pat myself on the back instead of beating myself up, because I know that if I'm patient I'll get there in due time.

A key part of practicing patience is setting goals. During my difficult convalescence, each literal step I took was a major milestone. Once the exertion was over and I had collapsed onto the sofa, I'd say to myself, "OK, you took 12 steps down the hall. Mission accomplished for today. Tomorrow you'll take 14." It may not sound like much, but that tiny increase every day motivated me to keep going.

Another huge take-away is the idea of connectivity. One event in your life can have a direct impact on others, even if it takes years for the connections to become clear. If I hadn't had Hodgkin's disease and excessive radiation, I never would have had coronary artery issues. Even though I rarely thought about my earlier illness – I had been "cured" 30 years before – that condition led me to my greatest challenge in life. So I look at my life now as a continuum, not as a series of unrelated events. You can learn so much about yourself and draw so much strength from your past. Don't dwell on what's done, or resent your bad breaks – let them help you be better.

The final, and maybe most important, lesson I learned is to take every detour without fear. Life throws us curves all the time. Just when everything is humming along perfectly, something pops up that throws us dizzyingly off course. It's not the event, but how we react to it, that determines how happily we live.

I think it's better to accept that life is not a straight road – we WILL have to change course many times – so try to enjoy the scenic route. Yes, it can be scary, but we have power over what we think and feel. Flood your mind with positivity and you may discover that the detour is more rewarding than staying on the original path.

As Robert Frost said of his choice between two roads, *"I took the one less traveled by, and that has made all the difference."*

STRENGTH

17. ROAD TO RECOVERY

After that grueling seven-hour surgery, I remember lying in the recovery room in a deep fog with a tube down my throat. I had never been so physically uncomfortable. I was trying to shake off the anesthesia but couldn't come out of my stupor. If you've ever been knocked out, you know how awful those first moments of consciousness can be. You want to wake up but the waves of sleep keep pulling you under.

Several hours later, I was in my private room and more alert. Unfortunately, I was beginning to feel the post-surgical pain, but the nurses were ready with syringes and IV drips. I can't say enough good things about the wonderful nursing team that took care of me – their dedication and professionalism, compassion and affection, got me through many difficult hours over the next few days.

The next morning, my day nurse told me that the Physical Therapy team was coming to help me move to a chair. I could not process this. Was residual anesthesia affecting my hearing? Move. To a chair. I can't even scratch my nose. My chest is stapled together. And you want me to get up?

Think about every individual movement your body has to make to sit up and walk. It's easy when you're healthy, but when you're not it's like scaling a mountain after a full day's surgery. I could not imagine how I would move my leg far enough to swivel my body into a semi-upright position. The idea of bending at the waist to stand was incomprehensible. While I had every intention of cooperating, I was not at all convinced that they could get this sawed-in-half patient moving.

The PT team was a very nice, extremely patient husband and wife. They explained that the first step to recovery was to get me mobile. I had tubes everywhere, was incredibly sore, and frankly, thought the whole thing was nuts. I wasn't being obstinate; it simply was too painful and required more energy than I thought I had. They assured me repeatedly – I'm guessing every five seconds – that I could do it, and coaxed me through every movement; just rolling over took five minutes. They pulled out every trick in the book, and inch by torturous inch they got me to sit up. I think they were determined to get me out of bed even if my liver fell out. Their persistence never flagged, but I'm sure by the end of that session they were more exhausted than I was.

One foot eventually hit the floor, then the other. It seemed as if I sat on the edge of that bed for hours wondering how on earth I was going to stand up and conduct my body to the chair way across the room. Once my behind was off the bed, I began the laborious shuffle to the other side of the room. It was probably all of 15 feet. It took more than 25 minutes, but I made it—quite a triumph for my first full day of recovery.

And that's how it went. Baby steps for a few days, a walker a few days later; from gelatin and broth, to oatmeal and soft eggs, to food that required chewing. Countless scans and blood draws ensured that my recovery was on track. After 10 days in Intensive Care and then a regular room, it was time to go home and continue the long process of reclaiming my health.

All the movements I had taken for granted – like getting in and out of a car – now took an excruciatingly long time to complete. Brian Wolf and Paul Bell helped – carried, really – me into the house and wanted to get me into bed. Simple enough, except that I had to make it up 13 steps (yes, I counted) to the second floor. I was barely able to lift my legs, so I took it step by agonizing step for all 13, with them fully supporting my weight. Reaching the bed took more than 20 sweat-soaked minutes. I'm not sure who was more worn out by the climb, my buddies or me, but we made it. I proudly added one more accomplishment to my growing list.

The next day, Scott came by after softball to check on me. I was relatively pain free, and all seemed to be on schedule except for one major thing: the staples Dr. Brown had used to close the cavern in my chest were coming apart. You could look into the opening and see my heart beating … absolutely amazing and shocking at the same time. Fascinating as it was, I could not live with a gaping hole in my chest. The potential for infection was the biggest immediate worry. The longer-term issues were too many to contemplate. Scott snapped a picture and emailed it to a plastic surgeon immediately.

Apparently, my chest wall was not strong enough to hold the staples and remain closed—another unanticipated side effect of the excessive radiation from my Hodgkin's treatment. So back to the hospital we went, this time to consult with the team of plastic surgeons. The doctors concluded that the only way to fix the problem was to surgically build up my chest wall by creating a "flap" using my own abdominal muscle and tissue. This procedure would take another full day of surgery, first to retrieve the healthy muscle and tissue and then to transplant it to my chest.

I had just come through a near-death experience and an arduous surgery. I had made it home, only to learn that I was going right back for the next round. I was fully engaged in recovery mode, but now I had to switch lanes back to surgery mode with no warning. It took all of my willpower to feel positive, but what choice did I have? I was determined to do whatever it took to get healthy, so I talked myself into believing it could work. I tried to think in small increments: get through this, then deal with that. It was the only way I could stay sane. The big picture was too vast to visualize in a single frame.

My forced optimism was overshadowed by uncertainty. The plastic surgeon was *hoping* he could do it, but really wouldn't know until he opened me up and saw how much chest wall he had to work with. If he could do the procedure, it would take 14 hours; if not, I would be back in recovery in about 45 minutes. Of course, we were hoping for the longer of the two options. If it didn't work, I wasn't sure where that would leave me. *How could I heal if my chest wouldn't close? How could I live?*

They wheeled me into the OR the next day. Six-plus hours later, I woke up in recovery again, one ab muscle short and a new chest wall in place. I remember that the Ravens-Redskins pre-season game was on in the background, but I was too out of it to catch more than the occasional word of play-by-play. I was thinking, "What's the score? What down is it?" But I couldn't keep my eyes open or my mind focused. That game is probably the only one I won't remember.

The same level of discomfort accompanied this round of surgery, but at least I knew that my recovery could begin in earnest. Or so I hoped. I wasn't sure, at that point, if I could take another major detour.

Don't get me wrong: I have never been more scared in my life than when I saw the staples pulling apart and heard that the flap procedure was not guaranteed to work. At the same time, I had no control over the situation. I had to let go and trust the experts. From that moment on I decided I wouldn't worry until I absolutely had to. Anticipatory worry wastes time and saps your energy. Believing in a good outcome and staying positive until you know otherwise can soften the occasional bumpy landing.

You can create all kinds of scenarios in your mind, but until the reality is in front of you, your plans may be useless. Save yourself the time and turmoil until you're sure of what lies ahead. Then you can panic – but only for a moment. Allow yourself to think through bad news based on fact, not speculation. Ask questions, weigh your options, and make reality-driven – not what-if driven – decisions.

PHOTOS →

My wedding photo, May 4, 1986.

My first publicity photo for WBAL / 98 ROCK, 1986.

Enjoying a day on the golf course, early 1990s.

Attman's Deli Championship Team, 2001. Me, lower left.

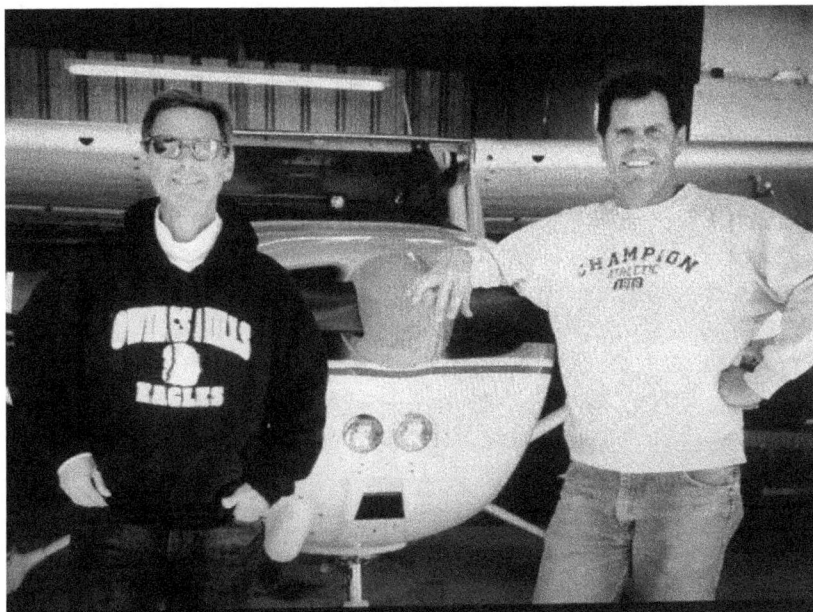

Me and Pilot Chip before another traffic flight.

Kings Championship Photo; 2005. Me: back row, far left.

Order from let to right: Brooks, Me, and Uncle Morris, during Alaskan cruise, enjoying some ice cream, August 2006.

Me about to hit a home run on a summer Sunday morning, August 2006.

Anual Turkey Bowl Football Game with my buddies, 2007. From Left to Right: Larry, Skip, Joe, Rick, and me.

My beautiful wife, Jody, soaking up the sunshine."

Proud to be an airplane owner, my traffic plane, 2008.

Up at bat before my collapse on the field; August 9, 2009.

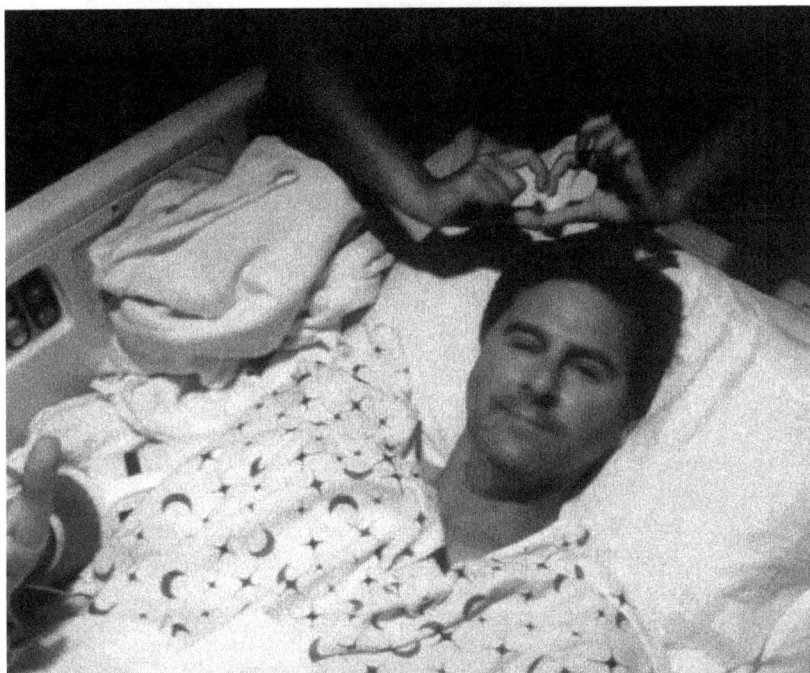

Me right before my bypass surgery, August 2009.

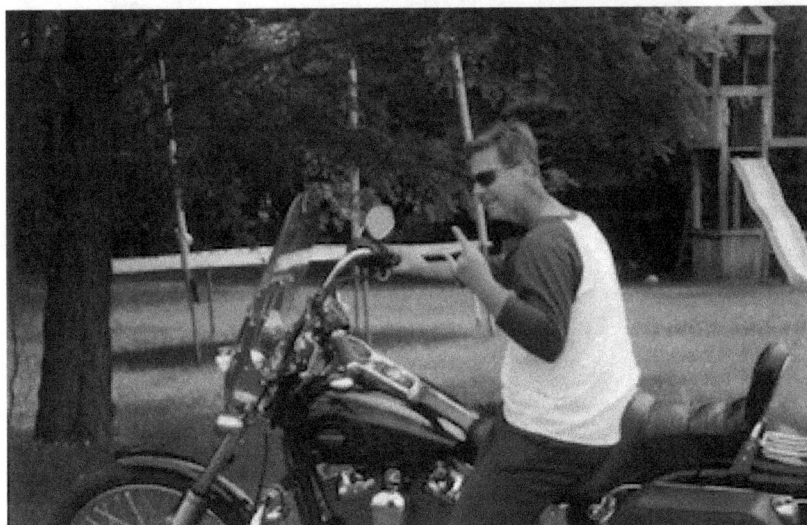

Me on my brother's motorcycle, after my bypass surgery, August 2009.

2009 Kings Team Picture, Three weeks after bypass surgery.
Brooks (back row, third from left), me (back row, middle)

Me cheering on my team at their 2009 League Championship game.

My beautiful family.

The doctors who saved my life. Order from left: Dr. Michael Herr, Dr. Scott Katzen, and me; March 2010.

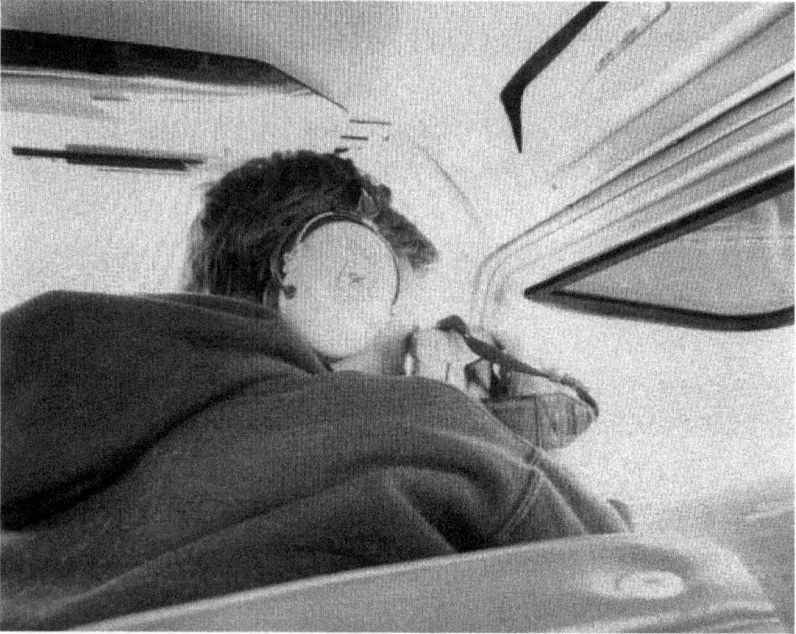

Me taking aerial photo over downtown Baltimore, Fall 2010.

Brooks and me, Displaying their championship trophy, August 22, 2010.

The women of my wife's family, From Left to Right: Alisa (Jody's twin sister), Sherry (Jody's mom), Alix (our daughter), Nancy (Jody's older sister), and Jody."

Uncle Morris and me, on a boat ride in Long Beach, CA; 2011.

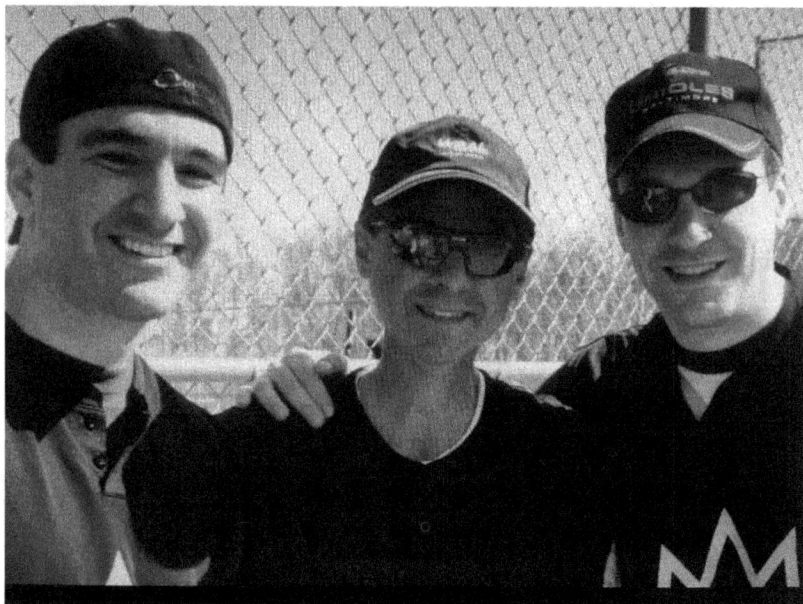

From Left to Right: Dr. Jan Katzen, me, Dr. Scott Katzen, Enjoying the game together.

Alix, Brooks, and me doing what we love at the Ravens game, 2012."

Order from left: Brooks and Alix, 2014. Celebrating Mother's Day.

My best friends: Rick Monfred and Joe Weinberg, 2014.

From Left to Right: Jody, Marty (Dave's stepdad), RosaLea (Dave's mom), and Dave, Enjoying Mother's Day.

Doug and me in the traffic center at WBAL / 98 ROCK, 2015.

My brother, Doug, and me, August 2015.

Alix and me at the Santa Monica, California mountain in 2015.

Me interviewing the Oriole bird at a wedding, October 2015.

YIELD

18. A NEW PERSPECTIVE

Before I got sick, I took an identical route to work every day. Every morning, at the ungodly hour of 4 a.m., I got in the car, turned the key, and off I went. It was just part of the daily grind. I was on autopilot. While I wouldn't suggest trying it, I'm sure I could have driven those roads blindfolded.

I didn't realize how much I was missing until I was forced to spend six months in the passenger seat. It was an eye-opening experience in every sense of the word. You might even call it life-changing.

During my recovery from my bypass and flap surgeries, I was not allowed to drive to and from appointments. When I finally got back to work I was weak and moving slowly. My doctors were concerned about my reflexes and the stress of fighting traffic, so they insisted that I let someone else take the wheel.

Not having to gas up the car or dodge the speed demons might sound sweet, but giving up control of the wheel wasn't easy. If you taught your kids to drive, you know what I'm talking about: pulling the seat belt just a little tighter, white-knuckling the overhead strap and pressing that imaginary brake for dear life. My "chauffeurs" had plenty of experience, so I wasn't scared – the truth was, I was struggling to accept my limitations. I wasn't fully in control of my life and my health, and that made me uncomfortable. Still, getting back to work even part-time was an important step, so I resigned myself to relying on others to get me where I needed to go.

Now, with the benefit of hindsight and a new perspective, I see how much I gained from sitting in the front right seat.

For the first time in decades, my eyes weren't jumping from the road, to the rearview mirror, to the side view mirror and back to the road. I wasn't preoccupied with merging cars, or blind spots, or menacing tractor trailers. Instead, I could look out the window and observe my surroundings. I could pay attention to everything *but* the traffic. The sights and sounds had been there all along, waiting for me to notice. I just hadn't had the opportunity.

I truly saw for the first time in years. The sprawling white clapboard house with the Palladian windows at the top of the hill was majestic. The yellow and pink flowers at the tight turn onto Greenspring Valley Road were in full bloom. I speculated about who lived at the ends of all those meandering driveways. I marveled at the age-old trees lining the roads like soldiers at attention. I wondered who tacked the hand-made protest sign, "STOP the development NOW!" to one of those trees. When had that red barn with the quarried stone foundation been rebuilt? Was that wrought iron weathervane always there?

I'd been oblivious to all of this detailed beauty, and one person's effort to preserve it, for years. What a pleasure it was to sit back and see the same old daily commute transformed into something fresh and engaging. What a lesson it taught me about taking the time to slow down and enjoy the ride. I finally had that chance, and I was going to relish every minute. My biggest regret? That it took a health catastrophe for me to realize it.

I encourage you to start looking for that balance in your own life today. How can you reorganize your time so that you spend less on the to-do list and more on the want-to-do list? Re-examine your life and make the changes that will make it even more rewarding. Find inspiration in simple things.

I would never suggest that anyone take their eyes off the road to daydream – I've reported on too many accidents in my career to put anything above vigilance. But having been a passenger for all of those months, I realized how much one misses during their daily commute. My advice? Every once in a while, relinquish control of the wheel. Let someone else be in charge. You'll gain a new perspective about so many things, most of which have been right in front of you all along.

Many of us think that giving up control is constricting, when it's actually just the opposite. Control is highly overrated. By that, I mean that we spend so much time trying to be right, to show others how competent we are, to micromanage events, that we don't fully explore our world and our relationships. Giving up control can be the most freeing thing you can do for yourself.

So kick back and savor what's all around you. You'll gain a new perspective about your world, your relationships, and yourself. Use that wisdom to remind yourself of what really matters, and to prioritize people and things in the proper order.

Try it. I guarantee you'll like the view.

PERSERVERANCE

19. A STEADY PACE

By the spring of 2010, I was feeling pretty good. My nine-month recovery from bypass surgery and the defibrillator insertion had gone well. I was back at work and DJ'ing on weekends. I had regained some weight and strength. I was ready to test my athletic limits, with medical approval, of course. I knew I didn't have enough wind to play basketball or run, but I thought softball might make the cut. I asked my medical team what they thought, and no one had any objections to my playing.

So, on a bright and sunny Sunday morning, the competitors gathered on the field. All the players, friend and foe, personally welcomed me back with handshakes, pats on the back and words of encouragement. Just being there was buoying my spirits, but their enthusiasm made me feel even better. There is something special about hanging with a terrific group of guys who play to win. It wasn't until that moment that I realized how much I had missed those Sunday mornings. I was stoked and ready to play.

The first couple of innings were intense, with both teams hitting well. By the time I was up, the score was tied, but I was confident that I could move us ahead. There was a man in scoring position with one out, and I was determined to bring him home. The slider crossed the plate and I swung as hard as I could. THWACK! I hit a long sacrifice fly towards right field. As I charged toward first, I suddenly felt dizzy and disoriented. I made it halfway up the first-base line before my knees buckled and I fell to the ground. I didn't pass out, and my heart was still beating, but something was very wrong. That hit was to be my first – and unfortunately, only – at bat of the season.

My cardiologist and hero, Scott Katzen, was in the stands again. Maybe he'd come out that day just in case I needed him? He and several players who are paramedics rushed over to me. They checked my vitals, and, taking no chances, sped me to the hospital. The exam revealed that I was suffering from bradycardia, an abnormally low heart rate. The condition means that, at times, the heart cannot pump enough oxygenated blood throughout the body. The normal resting heart rate is 60-100 beats per minute; mine was about 40. This probably was due to the Hodgkin's radiation, like all of my troubles. If it wasn't addressed, it could cause serious problems every time I exerted myself. No one could have anticipated this condition until I'd worked up a sweat, and I'd hardly moved for close to a year. Now we knew.

On the way out of the ER, Scott told me that the next step was to have a pacemaker wire attached to my defibrillator and to my heart. The device would be set to regulate my resting and active heart rates so that I would have adequate blood flow at rest, and could work up a sweat without triggering the defibrillator. He said the range would be 60 beats at rest and 180 beats during exercise. Once the wire was in, I'd be able to resume a reasonable amount of aerobic activity without collapsing.

I returned to University of Maryland Medical Center for the procedure about a week later. The surgery went well, and I was resting comfortably when I had a pleasant surprise. Ellen Beth Levitt, who had worked with me at WCBM years before, was now the director of public affairs and media relations for UMMC (she moved to Johns Hopkins Hospital in 2011). We kept in touch over the years, and shared another connection: her husband, Jackson Whitt, worked at WBAL as the station announcer, so she was aware of what had happened to me.

She stopped by my room with an intriguing proposal. "Dave, I've been thinking about your story. There are 100 guys in your league, and what happened to you could happen to any of them. What if we could use your experience to get a defibrillator donated to the Pikesville softball league?" I loved the idea. I told Ellen Beth that I would play my part. "If we can help one person avoid what I've been through, or save a life, that would be fantastic!"

Ellen Beth scouted potential sponsors and found an enthusiastic one in Chesapeake AED, a company that distributes Automatic External Defibrillators. Unlike my internal device, the AED is a compact unit that can restore a regular heartbeat during sudden cardiac arrest. No medical training is required to use it; the machine "talks" the user through each step. Many collegiate and high school teams now keep AEDs on the field to revive stricken athletes. I figured that if 11-year-olds were at risk, the senior leaguers definitely needed an AED within reach.

With a sponsor in place, Ellen Beth planned a dedication ceremony that drew media from TV, print and radio to the softball field where I'd collapsed. She used my near-death experience as the back story, and I had an opportunity to speak about my surgeries and recovery. Chesapeake AED presented the machine to the head of the league, and it was given a prominent place inside the pavilion, just steps from the field. The event garnered a lot of attention, and I was grateful to have played a role in securing this life-saving device for everyone who played on those fields.

You might be wondering why, after multiple scares, surgeries and lengthy convalescence, I got back out on the softball field. Primarily it's because I have never been a quitter. There was no medical reason not to play—or so we thought—so I did what I always did in the spring: I played ball. Granted, I didn't get far, but I had to try. It's always better to test your limits and fail than to sit on the sidelines wondering whether you could have done it.

In saying that, I am also a realist. I took a shot and it didn't work out. That second episode convinced me that I had to find another way to be part of the team—not to quit, but to adjust my role and my expectations. Once the pacemaker was in and I was doing well, I volunteered to coach, pick up snacks, lug bats ... anything to contribute to the team. If I couldn't be on the field, being *at* the field was fine with me. It was no different than when I was a high school athlete and realized that I wasn't going to be the next Brooks or Boog. I aspired to become the next Chuck instead. That pivot kept me close to the action in a way that worked for me.

I miss playing but I'd rather be involved at 60% than not participate. If you can follow my math, giving 100% to the 60% you're capable of beats 0% every time. Accept your limitations and reinvent your role. You can still find tremendous satisfaction in showing up. There's no question in my mind that the guys value having me around – maybe it serves as a reminder of what one person can achieve with enough perseverance, or maybe I'm a first-rate first-base coach. I'm sure they miss my clutch hits, but at least they don't have to miss me. As long as I can participate, the camaraderie and competition will keep me coming to those steamy Sundays at the park.

STEADY

20. PULMONARY ISSUES POP UP

With my chest wall rebuilt and the flap holding, I thought the worst was behind me. Heart failure and two major surgeries in less than a month hadn't taken me out. I wouldn't use the word "invincible" to describe my mindset, but I was confident that my health was moving in the right direction. I felt pretty good following the second surgery, certainly much better than I had after the bypass. But in truth, I was a mess.

I left the hospital with about 25 fewer pounds on my frame. The weight loss wasn't a surprise: I had been in and out of the OR in such rapid succession; I'd been subsisting on liquids and gelatin for weeks. My muscles were atrophying from lack of nutrients and exercise, and walking more than a dozen steps took concerted effort.

In spite of my weak condition I wanted desperately to get back to work. I had been doing traffic for more than 20 years and I had no plans to stop anytime soon. Nothing, not even a near-death experience and collapsed chest wall, was going to keep Detour Dave off the air for long. I'm sure my bravado was psychological: if I was well enough to work, I was "cured," and it kept my anxiety over a potential relapse at bay.

During my convalescence, I kept in close contact with my News Director, Mark Miller. He needed to gauge my progress, and I guess I needed to hear that WBAL/98 ROCK still wanted me. We talked once a week; I always pleaded the case that I was ready to return, exaggerating how well I felt. It wasn't that I wanted to deceive Mark; it was more about me wanting to believe that I could still do my job after all the trauma I'd been through.

Mark would judge how well I really was based on the quality of my voice. No matter how much I insisted that I was ready to go, he'd reply, "Sorry, Dave; it doesn't sound like it to me. Let's see how you sound next week." What Mark heard, and what I didn't want to acknowledge, was that my voice was greatly diminished because I was too weak to project. The diaphragm is a muscle, and mine was working at about 40% capacity. At first I attributed it to the tube that had been in my esophagus during surgery. Once the tube is withdrawn, it takes a few days for the irritation in your throat to subside and for your voice to regain its normal tone. But after several weeks of failing to persuade him, I had to admit that the tube wasn't responsible. Something else was going on, and no matter how firmly I denied it, my voice told the true story.

During this same period, I visited the plastic surgeon several times to ensure that his handiwork was holding. A visiting nurse came to the house a few times a week to check on my vitals and the staples. All was looking good, which in some respects was more frustrating for me. I hated sitting around, even though I barely had the strength to make it up and down the stairs. I hadn't fully accepted how frail I was. The bright spot was Mark's constant assurance that the stations were in no rush to put me back on the air prematurely. "We've got it covered, so just focus on recovering," he said.

The push-pull continued between Mark and I for another month. I would try to sell him on the idea that I was ready to return, and he would explain why I wasn't. My voice sounded weak and thin, and he didn't want to put me on the air. He was concerned about me, but also concerned about how listeners would react to my anemic sound. He reiterated on every call that I should take all the time I needed to get well. Of course I would never take advantage of the situation, but it was so comforting to know that I could come back when I was strong and healthy enough to do the job well.

While I recuperated, BAL provided fill-in talent and continued to compensate me, which was a huge relief. Remember that I wasn't an employee with sick leave, but an independent contractor; the station was under no obligation to pay me. Their generosity was overwhelming, and I get emotional to this day when I think of how loyal and compassionate they were during my initial convalescence. I felt wanted, and that contributed immeasurably to my recovery.

The station's patience notwithstanding, I had some pretty dark moments, both physically and psychologically. The illness and surgeries had depleted my body, and I often questioned whether I would ever improve enough to resume working. I was a relatively young guy – not even 50 – and I was not ready or willing to live the rest of my life as an invalid. But as I struggled to walk 20 feet from the kitchen to the family room, I couldn't help thinking that this could be as good as it got.

On those bleak days, the overwhelming outpouring of letters, emails and Facebook messages from listeners and clients was a tremendous mood-lifter. The volume got so crazy for WBAL that they created a special page on their website where people could send their well wishes. Jody read them to me daily, and we tried to respond to everyone. I felt blessed to have so many people in my corner; those messages showed me that my fans wanted me back on the air and that I hadn't been forgotten.

Another month passed, and finally Mark heard what he wanted to hear – and so did I: BAL would ease me back onto the air slowly for a few hours a week. There would be no getting up at the crack of dawn, no rigors of the rush hour just yet, just some easy mid-day reports as I worked up to full-time. That was their game plan. They would dictate the pace. All I needed to do was follow the playbook and continue to build my strength.

When I got the news I was like a little kid surrounded by his mountain of Halloween candy – I couldn't wait to dig in and eat the entire haul. I was feeling more robust, and my voice was clearer and less breathy. Having Mark acknowledge the improvement meant I had cleared the final hurdle. The long months of recovery were the most sedentary of my life, and I'd had enough. Every afternoon I happily climbed into the passenger seat, eager to get behind the mic and interact with listeners and program hosts again.

Over the next five months my hours increased gradually – yes, it took almost half a year for my voice to sound strong enough for the afternoon rush. Everyone was optimistic that I could resume working full-time; medically I was sound, and the station was pleased with my progress. My biggest challenge was shortness of breath, but I managed to mask it when I was on the air. I asked Scott why this was happening, and he explained that the heart surgery had caused me to retain fluid which diminished my lung capacity. He expected it to lessen over time, but as the weeks went by there was no improvement. When the fluid built up to a certain level I felt like I had run a sprint and couldn't fully inflate my lungs. If you've ever waited a few seconds too long to come up for air when swimming, you know the feeling.

Because my body was unable to expel the fluid on its own, Scott suggested that I see a pulmonologist at UMMC. Over the next seven months I underwent five thoracentesis, during which the doctor inserted a needle directly into my lungs to withdraw fluid, kind of like a needle biopsy. Unfortunately, I did not achieve permanent relief, so he referred me to a pulmonology specialist at Union Memorial Hospital.

After my first exam, the specialist recommended inserting a small drain into my side to which I could attach a vacuum that literally sucked the fluid out of my lungs and deposited it into a plastic bottle.

The good news was that I could drain the fluid myself at home instead of in the hospital. The bad news was I had to drain the fluid myself at home with assistance from Jody. He taught us how to do it, and we went home with our mini "Hoover" and a carton of disposable bottles.

Like clockwork, I felt the fluid building up every two or three days. I became increasingly short of breath, and it was time to drain. To give you a sense of how much fluid I retained, I lost two to three pounds after every treatment. The vacuum removed about a half-liter of liquid, which is about 17 ounces, or roughly one bottle of soda. Who would have thought that I'd look forward to attaching that vacuum and forcing fluid from my body? I felt so much better once it was done; it became the highlight of my day.

Between treatments the fluid weighed me down, literally. I struggled to walk for long stretches. Climbing two flights of stairs to reach the studio was like scaling Mt. Everest. Before I got sick, I could run up those stairs with air to spare; now I had to stop several times to catch my breath. That was a frightening daily reminder of how limited my lung capacity was. Every time I paused on those stairs I asked myself, "How are you going to punch out traffic reports every 10 minutes when you can barely make it up 10 steps?"

I continued the cycle of going to work, doing the occasional DJ gig, draining my lungs, and trying to live as fully as possible. I knew that I was lucky to be alive, lucky to have such a supportive family and workplace, lucky to be well enough to work. But I wasn't thriving. I had a plastic tube taped tightly to my abdomen. It could clog in the shower; it had to be pristine to avoid infection – it was the proverbial thorn in my side. It was keeping me functional, but it was also a constant reminder of my year-long ordeal. I wanted to feel well, to be well, and I wanted some answers about how to get there. I needed this pulmonary issue to end.

This period was the most difficult part of my recovery because I was in a kind of limbo: not sick enough to be in bed, but not well enough to function at 100% – and at that point I would have settled for 60% of where I'd been before the collapse. Frustration was a frequent emotion during those challenging months, and it took effort to retain my usual optimism. I don't ever recall saying "Why me?", but surely it was in the back of my mind. I'm only human.

To keep my spirits up I reminded myself that the surgeries had removed the major roadblocks to my recovery. My heart was working, I was getting stronger, and my lungs were functional. I had so much to be thankful for. Give it time. Give it time.

I soon learned that no amount of time would improve my breathing capacity. It would take far more intensive medical intervention to fix my debilitated lungs.

CALL OUT BOX: Here's how one listener created a post in my honor using my traffic reporter voice. Note how he squeezed in every conceivable traffic term.

"The_Man posts: I love Detour Dave. He does a great job and genuinely seems to care about helping people get home to their families as quickly and safely as possible! So here's a little tribute:

Hi, Detour Dave here. Looks like we've got a severe jam in my coronary artery. There's a bunch of plaque in the roadway causing a lot of stop and go flow of blood to my heart. A good alternative route will be for surgeons to take a healthy blood vessel from elsewhere in my body and use that to make a detour around the blockage. That ought to have me back up to speed in no time!"

FAITH

21. BACK TO THE HOSPITAL

The twice-weekly cycle of dragging through my daily tasks and draining fluid went on for a few months. The discomfort was interfering with every aspect of my life, and the relief was short-lived. I knew that I could not continue like this for the long haul; we had to find a more permanent solution.

I returned to the doctor and told him that I wanted the tube out. I asked him, with some desperation in my breathy voice, if there wasn't another approach that might eliminate the fluid once and for all. He said, "There's a procedure called pleurodesis that's often used with lung cancer patients. It might work if you're willing to undergo another operation."

He explained that there are pleural spaces between the lungs and chest wall where excess fluid can collect. If the body is unable to expel the fluid naturally, as was my case, the fluid constricts the lungs, making it hard to breathe. He then walked me through the procedure step by step. He would start by draining the fluid, after which he would surgically obliterate the spaces between the pleural layers of the lungs. No spaces, no fluid. Often a solution containing talcum powder is injected into the area; he agreed to skip this step, as it offered no clear benefit to me.

After discussing the pros and cons with Scott and my family, we agreed that pleurodesis was the best option. I was miserable and willing to try anything. I refused to consider the possibility that it might not work. The tube had to go, the fluid had to go, and if it meant another operation, so be it.

A week after the consultation, one of the doctor's associates performed the surgery at Union Memorial Hospital. The procedure itself was relatively quick, and for the first few days post-surgery, I felt good physically. There was minimal pain. Best of all, the hated tube and vacuum were gone. I began to imagine all the things I would do again, simple things that most of us take for granted: walk a flight of stairs, shop for groceries, play with our dogs, talk for more than five seconds without feeling out of breath. I wasn't asking to run a marathon or even to play softball again. I just wanted to live to the fullest at the highest capacity I could achieve.

I returned home filled with hope that my long ordeal was coming to an end. But a few days later, out of nowhere, my breathing became labored. I could hardly catch my breath, and activity of any kind made me feel as if I were drowning. It was obvious that the procedure was not working. I wheezed to Jody that we needed to go to the hospital. I have no idea how she held it together long enough to make that drive. I'm not sure I could have done the same had our roles been reversed.

I was readmitted to Union Memorial and underwent another cardiac catheterization to rule out a heart issue. Thank goodness my ticker was working well. So what was the problem? Despite multiple tests and consultations, no one at Union could figure it out. All the docs who saw me concurred that I needed a lung specialist to diagnose and treat me. They made a few calls to Johns Hopkins, one of the world's leading medical institutions, and within hours I was on my way to see Dr. Stephen Yang, a renowned thoracic surgeon. The doctors assured me that he would be able to fix whatever was causing this new issue. I held on to those words like they were gold. If he couldn't resolve it, what hope was left for me? Would I be tethered to an oxygen tank for the rest of my life, a cannula in my nose? Dr. Yang had to have the answer.

I am not a superstitious man by nature. I don't believe in curses. I don't deny that there may be supernatural forces at work in the universe, but if I don't see them, I don't give them much credence. But I have to confess, at this point, "cursed" felt like the precise adjective to describe me. Every time an end to my medical troubles was in sight, WHAM, another setback. *Had I done something to deserve this? Was this some kind of cosmic payback?* I was grasping for answers, and since the medical establishment was coming up empty, I started contemplating other possibilities. Maybe there were forces at work that I didn't understand. Maybe this was how the rest of my life was going to play out, running from one hospital to another, one doctor to another, in a fruitless search for a cure.

Jody's cousin Dorrie volunteered to drive with us to Hopkins. Jody definitely needed the moral support, and I was glad she would have company while I completed the reams of registration paperwork. As we approached the sprawling Hopkins medical campus I tried to remain positive. This was Hopkins, source of countless medical miracles; surely there was something in those hallowed halls for me?

After waiting five hours for a bed to become available, an orderly wheeled me to a cold, cavernous semi-private room in the old part of the hospital. Although I could not have cared less about the accommodations, the gloom made an already-depressing situation worse. As a nurse helped me into a gown, I saw how much my body had wasted. I was exhausted, and couldn't wait to climb into the bed.

The head of cardiology came in shortly thereafter and towered over my shrunken form. His bedside manner was detached and cold, which was not what Jody or I needed at that point. I've never run from the facts, but as the saying goes, "it's not what you say, it's how you say it." He had no time (or capacity?) for compassion. He reviewed my case in a brusque, clinical tone, droning on about the radiation I'd had for Hodgkin's disease and the bypass. The longer he went on, the farther I drifted. I knew all of this – could he just jump to the part about how they were going to fix my lungs? He sounded like the teacher in the Charlie Brown holiday specials, a jumble of unintelligible trumpet sounds, until a single, terrifying phrase broke through: "Mr. Sandler, your prognosis is not good."

My mouth went dry, my stomach dropped, and I felt tears forming. I struggled to keep my emotions under control. To be honest, I can't recall exactly what I was thinking at that moment. I was pumping adrenaline and couldn't get my mind to work properly. I'm sure I thought, "This guy is a real bastard for being so indifferent about my life," or words to that effect. I was worried about Jody and the kids. My worst fear—living like a faded version of myself for the rest of my days – hit me like a speeding tractor-trailer. I was only 49 at the time. This was a roadblock for which I was utterly unprepared.

Once he finished his ominous monologue, I took comfort in knowing that I wouldn't see him again. He may have been a terrific clinician, but I needed someone with a bit more heart (how ironic for a cardiologist). Scott was still on my team; everyone else I'd met at Hopkins was kind and caring, and I'd heard nothing but great things about Dr. Yang. I pulled myself together and decided to wait for all the data to come in before I spent any more precious energy worrying.

DRAINING

22. A GLIMMER OF HOPE

Within two hours of that initial unsettling consultation, Dr. Daniel Judge paid me a visit. He introduced himself as the cardiologist who would handle my case in conjunction with Dr. Yang. Surrounded by a team of med students and interns, he put me at ease instantly. He came across as extremely knowledgeable and competent, but not egotistical. I was impressed by how he taught the students while paying attention to what I told him. His compassionate bedside manner lifted my spirits immediately. He understood me and knew exactly how to speak to me. We were going to get along fine.

Based on my chart, he offered a few different scenarios without raising undue alarm. Even though he couldn't be definitive about anything at that point, I had to ask the big questions: *is this life-threatening? Will I ever lead anything close to a "normal" life again? Is my career over?* He was quick to reassure me. "You have been through so much, you deserve a break. I believe that we can get you back up to speed so you can get on with your life." Those words of encouragement, while not a promise, kept me going during the next few days in the hospital.

The cardiac catheterization at Union Memorial had ruled out heart issues, so Drs. Judge and Yang concurred that the problem was pulmonary. To pinpoint the precise cause, the first step was to remove all the fluid through a procedure called diuresis. I took a high dose of urine-producing medication for several days, which sent me to the bathroom every 15 minutes or so. It was disruptive, to say the least, and I'm surprised the floor tiles didn't erode from how much I walked back and forth. I lost even more weight from my skeletal frame, another unwelcome side effect. But as the fluid began to dissipate, my breathing began to ease. This inspired even more confidence that my new medical team had a clear direction—just what this weary traffic guy needed to believe.

After three days of non-stop peeing, my lungs were clear enough for X-rays and a CAT scan. Drs. Judge and Yang reviewed the films to see what shape my lungs were in, an impossibility when they were drowning in liquid. Dr. Yang, who would make the call for or against surgery, came in that afternoon to share what they'd found. He showed me the films and told me that my right lung was in rough shape. While most of the fluid was gone, the lung was filled, for lack of a medical term, with gunk the consistency of wet cement. The weight of the goop had almost collapsed my lung, making it next to impossible to take in sufficient air.

This explained why I couldn't breathe, but what was this cement-like mess clogging up my airways? As Dr. Yang reviewed the procedures I'd had up to that point, he mentioned that pleurodesis typically includes injecting a talcum powder solution to irritate and close the space between the pleura where fluid accumulates. I remembered that. I also remembered asking specifically that it not be done. Apparently it had. The muck in my lungs was the talc.

At that moment of clarity I had a choice: to get mad or move on. I was so relieved to have a definitive answer—I chose the latter. My life and health were in Dr. Yang's hands now, and I believed that he could, in his words, "fix" me. Looking back would solve nothing. Being angry would not enhance my healing. My focus was on the present and the future. I let it go.

Now that I understood what caused my condition I could focus on the upcoming operation. I peppered him with questions about what he planned to do and what I could expect post-surgery. His plan was to deflate the lung, scrape it clean, rough up the pleura so no more fluid could collect, and re-inflate the lung. He was guardedly optimistic, but cautioned that everything could change once he "got into my chest and had a good look around." I suppose that I was hoping for a guarantee, but I had to be content with his promise that he would do his best to fix me. I liked the word "fix." To me, it equated to real recovery, not just another patch until the next crisis occurred. He assured me that he had seen worse, and encouraged me to stay positive. I would get excellent care at Hopkins, and while the recovery would take time, he believed that we were on the right path at last.

He wanted to put me on the surgical rotation as quickly as possible, but there was a wrinkle, this time on my end: I had scheduled a holiday party several months before, and the hosts really wanted Detour Dave to emcee. I felt obligated, even as I lay emaciated in that hospital gown, gasping for breath, to do the party. Everyone thought I was crazy – maybe I was, or maybe it was a way of feeling normal under those abnormal circumstances.

I bargained with the hospital staff. They agreed to let me go to the party as long as I came back immediately at the stroke of midnight. They had big plans for me, and I was not to skip town, stop for gas, or delay my return under any circumstances. I promised not to lose my glass loafers in the hotel lobby. With that solemn oath and a good laugh, they discharged me for the night. The surgery would be on Tuesday, giving me two days to rest.

I labored into my tux, which hung on my thin frame like a father's suit on a little boy pretending to be a grown up. Jody had to button the shirt for me, I was so weak. I brought an oxygen canister with me just in case. My entire family caravanned to the Sheraton Hotel in Columbia, MD to carry the equipment and set up – there was no way I could lift more than a CD or two.

When we got to the hotel I stashed the oxygen under my draped table so none of the guests could see it. Any time I felt short of breath, I'd duck my head and take a hit of pure O$_2$. My temporary roadies, Brooks Alix and Jody, propped me up all night. It was like watching "Weekend at Bernie's", although I was slightly – and I mean slightly – more animated than the titular character. The clients and guests knew I'd been ill, so my fragile appearance wasn't a shock ... or if it was, they were gracious enough not to let on.

Despite some occasional hitches in my voice, I paced myself and made it through the final dance. Fortunately, it was a party with few announcements. I'm not sure I could have handled a wedding, but a simple celebration where all I had to do was wave and push buttons was doable. As always, Team Detour kept the party going. Remember the DJs' mantra about eating? Make that breathing.

Did hubris make me put on that tux and shuffle out to Columbia on that cold winter night, entourage in tow? I like to think that I'd have found a replacement if the job was too much for me. Doing the party for selfish reasons would have been unfair to my clients; they expected me to hit a home run, and I wouldn't do less.

Speaking of home runs, maybe I had Cal Ripken's record-setting streak on the brain. It was the year he'd set the record for playing 2632 consecutive games, a feat I admired deeply. I often thought about how he got up every day, did the job and didn't complain. I tried to emulate his dedication in my own work.

Or maybe, after all I'd been through, I needed to pretend to be the old Detour Dave, if only for one night. Whatever made me leave the hospital, I did so with a glimmer of hope, thanks to Drs. Judge and Yang. There were no guarantees, but I was still in the game, not complaining, hoping that my streak wasn't over.

RELIEF

23. PULLING THE PLUG

With my party obligation complete, I returned to Hopkins as promised and moved to the Harry and Jeannette Weinberg Center for the next phase of treatment. This comprehensive, state-of-the-art facility houses multiple medical departments, surgical suites, and patient rooms. Compared to my dim dungeon in the old part of Hopkins it felt like the Ritz-Carlton.

Maybe it was the sunny room, or my new medical team, or the unshakable support of my family, but I had a renewed sense of optimism despite all the unknowns. *How long would I be there? Would this latest surgery get me back on my feet for good?* I had no idea, but I was determined to let things run their course. No sense trying to control any of it. Dr. Yang was in charge from this point on. He stopped by the night before my surgery to reiterate that he would "clean up for good" all the crap preventing me from breathing normally. I went to sleep that night with a clear head and a hopeful outlook.

It might sound hard to fathom, given the gravity of my illness, but I was worried about how my absence was affecting the station. BAL had been scrambling with fill-in talent, but who knew when I'd be able to come back? They needed a long-term sub. I had heard through the broadcast grapevine that Jim Russ, a veteran Washington, D.C. traffic reporter, had lost his job. I contacted him to see if he was interested in taking my spot while I recuperated. He was delighted to hear from me, and he called WBAL. They quickly grabbed Jim before anyone else did, and my slot was covered. I was glad to help out a fellow broadcaster and the station until I could return to the air (that move came back to bite me later, but at the time it felt like the right thing to do).

With that hole plugged it was time to "fix that lung, fix that lung!" I actually chanted that on my way to the OR. For the next eleven hours, Dr. Yang deflated, scraped, and re-inflated my damaged right lung. He cleared out the wet cement that had constrained my breathing, and there was plenty of it. Normally he would have opened me from the front, but my rebuilt chest wall was too fragile. The flap had to remain in place undisturbed, so he flipped me over and made a deep incision though my back and around my right side. The unorthodox entry made the procedure more complex for him and promised a more arduous recovery for me. But Dr. Yang's skill compensated for the added difficulty, and he exited the OR satisfied that he'd fixed me for good.

When I came out of the anesthesia several hours later, I was in excruciating pain. For three days I stayed in the ICU, where a team of dedicated nurses provided round-the-clock care and did their best to keep me comfortable. My family was there in shifts so I was never alone. My step-sister, Nancy, gave me soothing neck and back massages. Physical therapists came in daily to take me through breathing exercises designed to clear my lungs after surgery because—you guessed it—excess fluid can build up. To help my body expel the fluid, I receive a steady stream of medications as well.

On the fourth day they moved me out of the ICU and into a private room. I took this as a sign that I was making significant progress. I complied with all of the directives and worked as hard as I could to hasten my recovery. The medical team was pleased, so Jody, the kids, and extended family finally felt free to go home for much-needed sleep and showers. Then, on the seventh day, something went horribly wrong. God may have been resting, but no such luck for me. The scariest moment of the entire ordeal was about to strike, suddenly and without mercy. For the first time since the collapse I thought it was my time to go.

As I sat on the edge of my bed, proceeding through my breathing exercises alone, I started to feel dizzy and nauseated. I was gasping for breath, as if a piece of food was lodged in my windpipe, and then I could not get any air at all. It felt like my head was in a plastic bag – there was zero oxygen. I blacked out.

Thank goodness a nurse saw me and called a Code Blue—perhaps to match the color of my face?

As they sped me down the hall to the OR to suction my obstructed airway, Dr. Yang called Jody and told her to bring the family to Hopkins immediately in case I didn't make it. The kids were in school and there was no time to waste. Her friend Darla rushed her to the hospital and by the time they arrived I was out of danger. Dr. Yang had inserted a breathing tube to enable me to get as much air as possible as quickly as possible – they were not taking any chances on my own pulmonary apparatus. The breathing tube would stay in until Dr. Yang was certain I could breathe on my own.

He later explained to me that I had almost choked to death on a mucus plug, a collection of lung secretions that had solidified and lodged in my esophagus. If I had been able to breathe or cough deeply after surgery, I might have expelled it on my own. I couldn't, so the plug got larger and larger until it completely cut off my oxygen. I like to think that even while God was resting, He had one eye open in my direction; I had dodged yet another bullet and lived.

Would I seem ungrateful if I complained just a little about the breathing tube? If you've never had the displeasure, believe me, it is horribly uncomfortable. Ironically, your breathing feels labored, and you can't talk or eat. The only way I could communicate was by writing. My wrist and fingers were cramping from trying to keep up with the conversations swirling around me. I kept writing the same question 'til it filled every page: "When is this stinking tube coming out?"

Several hours later I heard a group of doctors conferring outside my room. One was trying to convince the others that the tube should come out. I wasn't sure who he was, but he was my new best friend. In my head I was rooting like crazy for him to win the argument. My brain waves must have penetrated because they concurred that the tube could be removed.

As uncomfortable as the tube was in my throat, it was even worse on the way out. Talk about a bizarre experience. The nurse instructed me to cough as hard as I could and keep blowing out until she removed the tube. The pushing and blowing reminded me of Jody giving birth, although her huffing and puffing lasted much longer. Still, I felt like I had just coughed up my newly repaired lung. That would have been a tragedy after all that surgery and the mucus plug fiasco.

The second that damned tube was out I started laughing and couldn't stop. The rush of emotion was overpowering. The past 24 hours had been a nightmare, but I was alive! Little things, like talking to your wife and kids, being able to swallow, to smile, felt huge to me. I finally believed that the worst was over. I was right, as far as my health was concerned, but I had many more barriers to negotiate in the months ahead as I struggled to get back on my feet.

PATIENCE

24. FINAL OVERTIME IS FINALLY OVER

Once the breathing tube was removed, the staff kept a close eye on me to ensure that there were no additional complications. As soon as they trusted that I was out of danger, they moved me out of ICU and into a private room. The nurses kept watch around the clock until my discharge. As much as I appreciated the extraordinary care, I hated all the procedures, the noise, the lack of privacy, the gown—as the saying goes, a hospital is no place to recover.

The routine never varied. A new face came in at around 7 a.m. and introduced him/herself as my nurse for the day. This nurse woke me every few hours to check my vital signs and draw blood. I tried to nap in-between the blood pressure checks and needle sticks. The respiratory therapist administered my breathing treatment. Oh, and there was an X-ray tech who thought he was a stand-up comedian. He came in a few times a week at 4:30 a.m. and treated me to a 90-second shtick that I watched in a stupor with one open eye – WAY too early to find anything remotely funny.

The highlight of the day – and this is so sad – was filling out the menu for my next meal. Will it be scrambled eggs and toast or pancakes? Turkey on wheat or a chef's salad? So many choices, so much time to think about them. The days of broth and gelatin were over, so visitors brought all kinds of treats, hoping I might start putting on some weight. I was allowed to eat anything I wanted, but I had no appetite. A friend brought me a fat, juicy corned beef sandwich on rye, and it took me a day and a half to finish it.

The hospital staff was kind, compassionate and caring, but I was exhausted. I yearned to see my front door, my yard, my trees – anything but the harsh lights and constant din of the ICU. More than anything I wanted to feel the soft sheets of my king-size bed as I drifted into a nine-hour, uninterrupted sleep.

The fact that I was starting to think about life after Hopkins was a good sign. Being in the hospital gave me a much-needed sense of security—no surprise given what I had gone through with the dreaded mucus plug. Now I wanted out, and that meant I was feeling better. What did the doctors need to see to convince them that I was ready?

Family and friends made sure that I had lots of company every day. I appreciated the fact they came, but the hospital atmosphere was getting to be too much. I had to get out of there. I had in mind the perfect goal for my liberation: the AFC Championship, Ravens vs. Patriots at New England, Sunday, January 22, 2012. I made my intentions known to Dr. Yang. He said that if my lungs were clear and my numbers were good, I was out of there. I also had to go to the bathroom regularly and demonstrate that I had enough strength to walk on my own. Talk about pressure! It was the end of the 4th quarter, the game clock was ticking and I had no timeouts left. But I was determined to score my freedom and be home in time for the kick off.

As game day drew closer, I realized that I wouldn't make my goal. I remember having a one-on-one talk with Dr. Yang on the Thursday before the playoff and falling apart completely. All of the strain of that last hospital stay came crashing in on me. I had held it together 'til that point, but when it seemed unlikely that I would be released, the emotions overwhelmed me. Recovering from the lung surgery was grueling, and I had almost died in the process. I had given so much blood I could have fed a family of vampires for months. I was poked and prodded constantly. I was sleep-deprived and barely eating. I wasn't sure how much more I could take.

As I tried to convey my feelings, I sobbed like a baby. I'm sure he'd heard this countless times from other patients and understood that I needed to vent until I couldn't cry any more. He listened sympathetically, then said all the right things: *hang in there, you are going to make it, this is the beginning of a fresh start for you.* We found the problem and fixed it for good. He gave me real hope and helped me see that I had turned the corner. All I needed was a little more patience. The talk was incredibly therapeutic, and from that point on, I had a renewed commitment to doing whatever was necessary to go home.

I worked doubly hard for the next couple of days, but by game time there I was, still in my gown in bed at Hopkins. Not what I had planned, but damn it, the Ravens were in it to win it and I wasn't going to miss a second of that contest.

I should mention that my favorite way to watch Ravens football is with my son Brooks. No parties, no sports bars. It's either with 70,000 of our closest friends at M&T Bank Stadium or at home in front of the big screen. As much as I wanted to share the playoff excitement with him, I convinced him to stay home. I knew that he hated the hospital, and I saw no point in ruining the game for him. To this day, it is one of the few games we haven't watched together. I knew he was disappointed so I promised him that if the Ravens were ever in the playoffs again, we'd go to the game together. But on this day nurse Linda was my companion through that crazy roller coaster of a game. She and I hunkered down in front of the tiny hospital TV and cheered the Ravens on.

If you recall, the game was back and forth all afternoon. My repaired heart was thumping out of my surgically reconstructed chest. My re-inflated lungs were huffing and puffing with each first down. Linda spent more time watching me than the game – I think she was worried I'd go into cardiac arrest. She had a point: when receiver Lee Evans dropped a potential touchdown ball, my defibrillator almost engaged. When kicker Billy Cundiff missed a 32-yard chip shot that would have sent it to overtime, they could have wheeled me back into the OR. Game over! I was wildly disappointed, but I survived intact with only a bruise to my Raven pride.

The Ravens were out of Super Bowl contention but the following day I was handed an even sweeter victory: Discharge! I met my goal, albeit a day later than intended. So, what's a little overtime in a situation like mine? Finally I was heading home to Reisterstown with **MY** team, Jody, Brooks and Alix. The Promised Land was just 20 minutes away, and my chauffeur, Jody, was on her way to pick me up.

I took off that flimsy gown and put on sweat pants for the first time in months. What a glorious feeling I got from that simple act. There were many of those triumphs over the ensuing weeks, and I call them triumphs without exaggerating. Making it up the stairs, tying my own shoes, tasting a favorite food, BREATHING – I would never take any of those pleasures for granted or complain about little things again. I was alive, I was on the mend, and every new thing I could do for myself felt like I'd won the Vince Lombardi trophy.

Real life was about to begin again. I had no idea when I would go back to work or if I still had a job. As Jody entered the room and said, "Let's go home," I could not have cared less.

If you follow football you know that the Ravens were in the play-offs the following year against, you guessed it, the Patriots. I wasn't well enough to go to the game, but I was certainly well enough to put on my Ravens gear and watch it in the family room with my football buddy, Brooks. The 2013 AFC Championship and subsequent Super Bowl win were more than enough to make up for that awful game I watched at Hopkins.

Fast forward to 2015. I'm writing this one week after returning from Foxboro, MA, where Brooks and I watched, in person, another matchup between the Ravens and the Pats, this time in the AFC

Divisional Playoffs. We drove six hours to Foxboro, sat for four hours in 16° weather, cheered the team's early lead, fumed over the loss, got back into the car, and drove another six hours back to Baltimore. That, my friends, is a road trip only a truly healthy man could survive. It was a long, but extremely gratifying, day on so many levels. The best part was fulfilling the promise I had made to my son from the hospital four years before. The Ravens lost the game, but Brooks and I headed home feeling like winners.

SUPPORT

25. IN THEIR OWN WORDS

My family was my rock during every phase of my illness and recovery. They rode the roller coaster with me, and I don't think I could have made it without them. Since I spent so much time under anesthesia or otherwise out of commission, I asked them to share their memories and the lessons they learned.

Jody:

For me, Dave's ordeal is bookended by two dreaded phone calls. The first was on that Sunday morning when he was on the softball field. It was only 9 a.m. so I wasn't expecting a call. I glanced at the caller ID and felt a little anxious as I picked up. It was a teammate telling me that Dave had passed out on the ball field, probably due to the heat; he was okay but was being transported to the closest hospital to be checked out.

Two things jumped out at me immediately: first, that our son, Brooks, who was with Dave that morning, hadn't called, and second, the idea that Dave would be affected by the heat. He played golf and softball no matter how scorching it was and barely broke a sweat. My gut told me that something much bigger was going on, but first I had to get to the hospital. Alix, our then-21-year old daughter, wasn't home, and I was too shaky to drive, so I called my twin, Alisa, to pick me up. While I waited for her I called Alix and our sister Nancy, who met us at the ER. On the drive I told Alisa what I knew, and we agreed that something wasn't adding up. I was trying not to panic, and she kept saying, "Let's just wait till we get there. Then you can panic."

Dave was lying in bed, fully alert, with a nasty lump on his head. They had scanned him to make sure he didn't have a cracked skull or fluid around the brain. The ER doc was nice enough, but I was upset that he wasn't trying to figure out *why* Dave had passed out. Brooks mentioned that they had done CPR on Dave, and that told me that his heart had stopped. Now I was really scared. It might sound crazy, but standing in that exam room, I understood that our lives were about to change—I just didn't know how drastically.

The second dreaded call was the one from Dr. Yang telling us to get to the hospital STAT because Dave might not make it through the episode with the mucus plug. It's hard to describe how overwhelmed I felt at that moment. We had been through so much: one illness after the other, Dave losing his job, the financial setbacks. We finally were seeing some light, and now *this*. I could not imagine how our family would go on. I have never been so scared about so many things. My mind was racing from one thing to another: the loneliness, how the kids would react, how we would survive financially. It was too much to process at once.

I think of Dave's illness like a yellow line down the middle of a road dividing how we lived before and after he got sick. Like most people, I guess we took a lot for granted. We didn't question where the next mortgage payment was coming from or whether he'd be strong enough to make it up the steps. We were secure in our friendships. Life was predictable and easy.

But as things were unfolding, everything we thought we knew turned upside down. We learned who our true friends were. I will never forget, or be able to thank enough, the people who rallied around

Dave, the kids, and me: my sisters Alisa and Nancy, my extended family, and close friends Barb Getlan, Gwen Hirsh, Darla Lansman, Linda Nachimson, Wanda Sizter and Jamie Verrecchio. I also could not have gone through any of this without my cousin Dorrie and my "substitute mom," Rita Shemer. All the kindnesses, large and small, got me through when I thought I couldn't take another setback. To Drs. Scott Katzen and Mike Herr, who saved Dave on that August morning, there are no words to express how grateful I am. They are forever in my heart.

While Dave's illnesses were the worst things that ever happened to us, our financial troubles were also painful. Early on it was hard for me to admit that we couldn't afford to do most of the things we'd done when Dave was earning a good living. I went back to work, but it wasn't enough to compensate for the income he had lost. Going from financial security to barely making ends meet showed me the importance of living with honesty. I learned to say "I can't" without embarrassment. I accepted it when supposed friends turned their backs because we couldn't keep up. It was humbling, but I am a better person for it. I discovered that there's power in paying cash. It taught me that when you're doing well you don't need to prove it with stuff, and when you're not you don't have to apologize for it. Handle what you can, but don't be afraid to ask for help. People can be incredibly generous if you let them.

It may be a cliché, but only because it's the truth: when you have your health, your family and wonderful friends, nothing else matters.

Alix:

I received the call from my mom on Sunday afternoon as I was lying by the pool at my friend's house. We had gone to a concert the night before and I ended up sleeping at her house after the show. My mom sounded upset. She said that my dad had been playing ball and suddenly passed out. I remember thinking it was pretty hot out, so that was the most likely cause. I mean, it was August and he was

40-something years old. He played every weekend but that was a boiling hot day. I asked her where he was and if I should come, thinking she would say, "No, it's no big deal." When she said, "Yes, he's at Northwest Hospital and I think you should come now," I figured something might be seriously wrong, but I stayed calm.

When I got to the hospital, I was taken back to his room in the ER. He was sitting up and looked fine, but there was a lot going on around us and a lot of waiting. Eventually he was transferred to the University of Maryland Hospital where there was even more waiting. I remember being calm the entire time, and my family thought this was interesting. I wasn't panicking; we knew nothing yet, so what was the point?

After sitting around for hours, the doctor came in with some test results. I remember my mom telling me that it was much worse than we thought. Something was going on with his heart, and he needed quadruple bypass surgery. My exact thoughts were: *what the hell? My dad's always been healthy. A heart issue? My mom always makes him go to the doctor. This can't be right.* I remember being on the hospital phone with my mom's friend when I heard the news, and I just started crying because I was so scared for him.

Now I was panicking.

I'm not sure why, but I don't ever remember feeling negative about the surgery or thinking that he wouldn't survive. I was definitely scared, though. I knew he was scared and no one really had the answers, but I cannot remember a time where I thought he wouldn't make it.

After the heart surgeries I started getting panic attacks pretty often. This was after he was home, but before we knew anything about his lung issues. I'm not sure why the attacks started, because I was pretty calm throughout most of the post-op events. I just remember having thoughts like *what would my mom and brother and I do without my dad? Would I be able to stay in school? Would we all get jobs and work to keep the house?* The uncertainty was the worst part. It's kind of ironic, because when we knew nothing at the beginning I kept it together. Now it was terrifying. I guess the panic attacks were the cumulative result of the entire trauma. I'm doing fine now, but it was a very unsettling period in my life.

I tried to stay busy by organizing all their mail, cleaning the house, making sure everyone was still happy and laughing, but I was scared. I wasn't sure how we would move forward normally after seeing my dad lying in bed for weeks, having trouble breathing and barely able to walk. Talking about financials with the family was annoying, frustrating and scary. I felt like I was too young to have these problems, and then felt selfish for only thinking of myself after seeing what my dad was going through. I was used to a guy who never even got a cold. He never took off work. He was always on the move, playing ball and going to work at one of his four jobs. This new reality felt unreal and impossible. It forced me to grow up faster than I might have wanted to, but we had to be honest and pull together to get through it.

After all of his heart and lung surgeries, I know nothing can bring my dad down. Each surgery was just another day for him. If he was afraid, he didn't share it. He remained positive even though it was a long hard year or so. I remember sitting in the hospital with him one night because he didn't want to be alone. That was a little odd for me, because I had never seen him that way. I was happy to be there, but I don't think I slept at all that night. I just made sure he was still breathing and wasn't going to wake up panicked from all the meds they were giving him. I played his favorite songs on Pandora, and he was able to smile and relax until he fell asleep.

I don't believe that our relationship has changed necessarily because of his illnesses. We have always been close and that remains the same. I DO know that the importance of family, for me, has changed. You can't let a moment pass without telling your family how you feel, good or bad. Your life can change completely in the blink of an eye, so you have to use every opportunity you have to express yourself. The only thing worse than losing someone you love is wondering if they knew how you felt.

Brooks

On the day my dad collapsed I remember being very confused, but not worried. I was only 16, so I don't think I fully understood what was going on or how significant it was.

I remember seeing him go down and thinking that he had passed out due to the heat and humidity. Not once did I think it was something that could be serious, or even fatal. I heard everyone yelling; Dr. Jan Katzen was screaming for his brother, Scott, who is a doctor, to come help. Everyone was gathered around my dad, or calling 911, or trying to figure out how to help.

I had moved onto the field, and I could see that they were working on him. I overheard either Mike, the team captain, or Scott say, "He has no pulse," but it didn't register until a few hours later. Another player grabbed me and led me away from the scene. He said that it wasn't a good idea for me to watch what was happening, but I didn't understand at the time why he said that. I later figured out that had my dad died, I wouldn't have seen it, which would have been less traumatic for me. Fortunately it didn't come to that. I think the scariest time for me was when we got the first diagnosis. Initially they thought he passed out and sustained a concussion, but the tests showed that it was a heart issue. Then I knew it was serious, and that he would have a long recovery. I was worried, and felt terrible for him, but there was never a time I thought he wasn't going to survive. Or maybe I didn't want to believe it. My dad and I are really close, so I just blocked out the idea.

I do remember being very emotional during the bypass surgery. I remember thinking that my dad was in a room with strangers who were solely responsible for him living or dying. Thinking about what could go wrong was horrible. Having no control over what happened in the operating room was an awful feeling. It was a very long wait for the results. It's a day I hope we never repeat.

I guess this experience changed me so that I now think, "If you want to do something, you should do it when you have the chance. Don't wait for another day, because that day may never come." Other than that I don't think that my life has changed as much as some would expect. I guess I cherish each day with loved ones a little more, but I never think about what would have been had my dad died. He recovered so I don't let my mind go there. At some point we all die, so I prefer to view the situation as a minor bump in a long road instead of some big deal. I do know that my dad and I have the same close relationship we have always had and that will never change.

Rosa Lea Finstein (my mom)

I always remember the time the DJs on 98 Rock called me wanting to know what certain Jewish expressions mean. I had no idea at the time that I was on the air, but those guys were always pulling pranks. One of the words they asked about was "tzimmes," which has two meanings. It's a traditional holiday food made with carrots and honey, but it also means a big deal, as in "don't make a big tzimmes about it." In other words, let it go.

I share this because it reminds me so perfectly of David. He never makes a tzimmes out of anything – cancer, heart failure, collapsed lungs. He always stays calm and positive. He's a fighter who never gives up. Through every surgery, every complication, he seemed so relaxed – I can't say what he felt on the inside, but the outside was always composed and together.

As his mother I tried to stay calm for him through every illness, but it wasn't easy. The possibility that you might lose your child is something no parent should have to go through. I was devastated to learn that he had cancer at age 20, scared to death, but admired so much what a fighter he was. From the beginning, he made it clear that there was no way this disease was going to get him, and he did what it took to get well.

The same is true for all the illnesses he faced because of the radiation. He just refused to give up, so I couldn't either. Even though it killed me to see him vomiting in the parking lot or rushing back to the hospital with another emergency, I kept a smile on my face. He was a good teacher in that respect. If I made a tzimmes out of it, it would have made him feel even worse. I just had to hold it together in front of him and cry in private.

The worst moment for me was when he came out of his last lung surgery. He was hooked up to so many tubes and wires I almost fainted. My heart sank when I saw him like that – he looked the worst I'd seen him after any surgery, and I remember thinking he might not make it. Thank God I was wrong. I don't know what I would do without him.

When I was a little girl, people saw me and said, "There goes Morris Bardolf's little sister." (That's Dave's beloved Uncle Morris, and my late brother, to whom he dedicated this book). Now people say, "There's Detour Dave's mother." When they find out I'm Dave's mom they go crazy. I guess it's because everyone likes him. He's so kind, so honest, and always civil. He's dedicated to his family and really cares about people. I think his personality is the secret to his success, as a person and in his professional life. He's just a wonderful young man, and I am so proud of him. My wish as his mother is to never, ever have to go through another health scare. Just live a long, healthy life and I'll be happy!

ATTITUDE

26. MEDICAL LIFE LESSONS

Hope. Trust. Positivity.

Those words were my anchors through every health crisis over that two-year period. I refused to abandon them, even when it seemed that medical science had abandoned me.

Hope sustained me whenever I encountered a new obstacle or hit a dead end. Hope kept me going when no one had any answers. Hope allowed me to accept without anger that mistakes had been made and to move on to the next potential solution. Sometimes the cure is worse than the illness, but we hope that the treatment, no matter how bizarre or painful, will restore us. If I had lost hope, I would have lost a reason to keep trying, to keep living. I hope I never get to that place, no matter what curve is lobbed in my direction.

Trust was harder to learn. It required relinquishing control, facing my fear of the unknown, and placing my faith in those with more knowledge, experience and wisdom. I had to trust Scott, whom I had just met, that moving to UMMC was best. I had to trust that there was something, anything, better than vacuuming fluid out of my body every two days. I had to trust that Dr. Yang could "fix that lung." Ultimately, I had to trust that I could heal. Belief in those who want to help you, and in yourself, can get you through almost anything. Letting go, letting it play out. When you stop struggling and start to trust, you find peace.

Positivity may just be how I'm hard-wired. I'm a sunny guy by nature, and that helped me through many dark and depressing days during those two years of illness. The chants on the way into the OR, the unwavering belief that I would get better, the refusal to give in to despair … who can say if they made an impact on the speed or extent of my recovery? I know that there have been studies about the mind-body connection; some say a positive attitude can change outcomes, others dispute that. Maybe it comes down to a choice about how you're going to make your way through a painful situation—pity party or positive outlook? Whether it's good science or quackery, I always choose to think the best. I'd rather err on the side of yes every time.

Now, even though I am not a superstitious guy, I need to add "guardian angel" to my list. I had way more than my fair share of luck. Did God have one eye open? Was there a soul who decided it wasn't my time to join the departed? Or was I just lucky to have some amazing, smart, loving people watching out for me?

When I went to the doctor about the lump on my chest I could have agreed to "keep an eye on it." But my mom insisted that we find out what it was. It saved my life. I dropped dead on the softball field, and Scott happened to be there. He and Mike saved my life. The Hopkins nurse who saw me lying unconscious when the mucus plug lodged in my throat saved my life. I mean, how many strikes does a guy get before he's out of the game? That's three right there, and there were plenty more during this saga. I cannot tell you why I was so fortunate. I cannot say why I lived to tell the tale multiple times. All I can say is "Thank you" to whomever or whatever thought I was worth having around.

All of this sounds a bit impractical, maybe slightly irrational. After all the medical trials, false starts and unanticipated turns, I accept that life is a crap shoot. We are just beginning to understand the human genome and the havoc mutations can cause at any point in our lives. Science will continue to evolve long after I'm gone. So I guess the best piece of advice I can share is to embrace and enjoy life, to weather the storms with as much grace and humor as you can, and to be grateful for every healthy day you're given.

SECTION 3

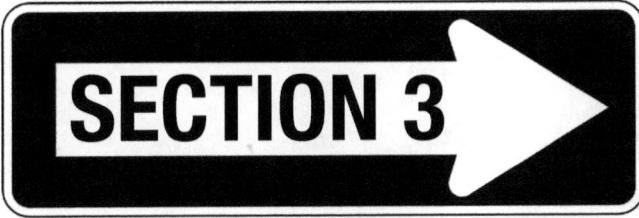

UNFORSEEN CONSEQUENCES
OF ANOTHER KIND

LOYALTY

27. HOME AT LAST

It felt incredible to be out of the hospital and on my way home. "Freeing" is the best word I can use to describe it. I was no longer tethered to tubes and wires and machines; the claustrophobia of being confined to one room most of the day and night disappeared as soon as the lobby doors opened. I was outside in the cold sunshine, watching people and cars and pigeons and belching smoke from Hopkins' operations plant. I smelled the snow and felt the wind against my face. It was beautiful.

As Jody turned onto the Jones Fall Expressway, I couldn't stop turning my head to look out the windows. That drive was one of the best I've ever taken. There weren't many cars on the road, but we could have been sitting in bumper-to-bumper traffic for hours and I would have been the happiest guy on the planet. I cracked the window to get a whiff of fresh air. I could breathe so easily with my newly repaired lungs. Amazing. I wasn't ready for sprints, but I wasn't gasping. In every respect I was headed in the right direction.

The next few days at home were peaceful. No one came in at 5 a.m. with a blood pressure cuff or thermometer (although I kind of missed the X-ray tech/comedian). Even though sleeping through the night remained difficult, I had plenty of uninterrupted nap time during the day. If you have ever had anesthesia you know what I mean. It takes a while for your body to return to its normal sleep pattern. But being home was all the therapy I needed. The healing could begin, and I believed that all my physical issues would eventually right themselves.

My weight was one of the first challenges. I had dropped about 30 pounds from my original 175, and I looked emaciated. My face was thin and my frame gaunt. My appearance was made worse by another residual of Hodgkin's called "lollipop head"; after radiation the neck narrows and the patient's head looks like a lollipop on a stick. I'm sure that when visitors saw me, they were shocked at how fragile I seemed. I guess that's why there was a non-stop flood of fattening foods – lasagnas, casseroles, brownies, cookies, you name it. Everyone was trying to put some meat on my bones, and we appreciated not having to grocery shop and cook. My appetite hadn't improved much, so I could barely eat more than a few bites before I was full. But the family ate extremely well.

I told Jody that for the next few months my priority was to regain weight and strength. Someone suggested milkshakes and protein drinks as great ways to pack in a lot of calories without much effort. I could nurse my daily smoothie for an hour and take in about 500 calories, versus eating four or five bites and consuming virtually nothing. Some of my closest buddies, like Rick Monfred and Joe Weinberg, came by regularly to take walks, shoot the breeze and share a few laughs. Seeing them, and all my visitors, raised my spirits. I was optimistic that, with a little time and rehab, I'd be back on the air soon.

During the seven weeks I'd been ill, I hadn't spent much time worrying about work – I'd had more serious issues to deal with. Mark Miller and the BAL management team had supported me so generously through my initial illness; even though Mark had moved on, I assumed that the same would hold true during this convalescence. But two weeks after I went home, I was blindsided by yet another major detour. I was enjoying a leisurely morning in my pajamas and was about to take a shower when Jody walked in and handed me the phone. "It's someone from the radio station," she said with a quizzical look on her face. We both knew that I rarely received calls from the station, so we both were curious.

On the other end of the phone was newly hired News Director Merrie Street. After we exchanged pleasantries, she took an audible breath and said, "Dave, I need to let you know that the station can no longer pay you while you are recovering. It's not personal. We have to provide traffic to our listeners, and we simply cannot afford to pay you while also paying a full-time fill in. I hope you understand."

She went on to say that they were going to make some changes. Jim Russ was going to take over my responsibilities for the morning and evening rush hours (you'll recall that I had introduced Jim to the station when he lost his job in DC a year earlier). Merrie added what I'm sure she thought was an encouraging note. "We'll consider you for vacation relief or fill-in work, but your regular shift is no longer available."

My stomach started to churn and my heart pounded. I had not been expecting this, or at least I expected to hear the word "temporarily" at the end of her announcement. I peppered her with questions. I didn't want to believe it, and thought that if I kept her on the phone long enough I could convince her to reverse the decision. I didn't know Merrie well and had a hard time reading her voice. After she repeated the verdict, I knew it was time to hang up. I needed to digest, and didn't want to say anything I might regret later. I thanked her for calling and told her that I wanted to speak with Dave Hill, the Program Director, for clarification.

As I put down the phone, my mind started racing. "I think I was just fired, but that couldn't be. I'm getting stronger … surely the station will allow me to get back behind the mic?" I'd been out almost six months the first time and they'd stuck with me; this time, not even eight weeks. The idea of losing a job I'd held for more than 20 years was terrifying. Remember, I had been doing traffic for WBAL since

1986. Being a traffic guy was all I knew. There were only a handful of jobs in the market, and they all were taken—including mine.

I turned to Jody, who had been listening to my half of the conversation and watching my facial expressions. I didn't need to say anything – she knew. Neither of us could believe it. I told her that this phone call wasn't the end of my career. "I'm going to set up a meeting with Dave Hill. I've known him for more than 10 years. He'll sort things out. Let's not panic until I speak with him." I called Dave immediately, but he was out of town and unreachable for a few days – not what I wanted to hear.

As I sat there, scared and dejected, a million thoughts ran through my head: *what if I'm done at BAL? How will I find work? I'm not well enough to interview. Even if I landed an interview, who would hire me looking like a bag-of-bones? How would we make it financially if I was permanently out of work? How could I focus on recovering with this hanging over me?* I was doing better but had a long, long way to go. Visions of a bleak future raced through my mind. I felt hopeless, and that's rare for me. But with so much working against me it was tough to stay positive.

Over the next few days I tried my best to keep it together, but anxiety was a constant presence. Dave was kind enough to return my call as soon as he could; he promised to meet with me to discuss the situation when he got back to Baltimore, but wouldn't confirm or deny that I was done. I had to be content with the promise of our meeting. He didn't sound angry at me, and he didn't say that his hands were tied. He simply said, "We'll talk when I get back." All of this gave me hope that a reversal was possible.

Still, I recognized that I **might** have to look for a new job. I emphasize the word "might," because the last thing I wanted to do was antagonize the station or make them look bad. They were protecting the franchise, something any business would and should do. Listeners expected accurate traffic reports on the 5's, and BAL needed someone to deliver those reports. Of course I wanted that someone to be me. My livelihood depended on them changing their minds and putting me back on the air. No one at BAL wanted to fire me, I was sure. I was well liked. I'd given them more than 20 years of dedicated, quality reporting and had contributed to building a successful brand. I remained grateful that they had carried me during my first illness. Nevertheless, my first responsibility was to my family. I needed to start networking.

What better venue than Facebook? I updated my page with the following post: "After 25 years I could be looking for a new opportunity!" No editorial comments, just the facts as I knew them. The response from listeners and friends was intense and immediate. "What do you mean?" "Did they let you go?" "We haven't heard you on the air in a while, what's up?" I didn't respond to any of the questions, even though it was tempting. I kept my mouth shut publicly because waging a negative social media campaign was not in anyone's interest.

Apparently what I intended with that post was not universally understood by the public or station management. A loyal fan assumed I'd been fired and created a "Keep Detour Dave on the Air" page. It went viral and soon had over 1200 comments. WBAL's General Manager, Ed Kiernan, got wind of it and sent me an urgent email indicating that my Facebook post was "damaging the station." I assumed that he was reacting to the fan page, and I had to agree that it created a PR problem for them. Even though my post was benign, I took it down and emailed Ed to that effect. I also apologized for "jumping the gun" on social media. I was looking for a job, not a fight. My search could wait until after the meeting with Dave and Merrie.

In the days leading up to the meeting I had a chance to reflect on what had occurred. I was struck by the similarity to my firing from Metro Traffic 20 years earlier. In both cases I had been let go. I was free to look for another job, but both employers were unhappy that I was doing so. Now, as then, it was a no-win for me. The big difference was the instantaneous impact of social media. In the past, negotiations were conducted among the stakeholders in private. Now, everyone with any interest in the story felt entitled to weigh in. I couldn't control the rumors or what others said or did, but I could control my words and actions. I decided that I would conduct myself in a dignified and objective manner, without assigning blame or fueling speculation. I would speak about BAL in a positive light at all times. It was the right thing to do, and I couldn't imagine handling myself in any other way.

Many people encouraged me to make my case in the media, and I certainly had plenty of inquiries. No doubt I would have garnered a lot of sympathy, but that would have meant violating my principles. I absolutely would not engage in public sniping with the station that had been so good to me over the years. To be honest, when I factored out the death blow to our finances, I had a hard time being angry about it – hurt, yes, but not angry. They had a business to run and a bottom line to manage. When I put myself in their place I understood their position completely.

I did consent to one brief interview with *The Baltimore Brew*, an independent, online daily release covering regional politics, media, education, and a host of other topics. Two days after Merrie's call, I responded to their question about the "firing" this way:

In a phone interview yesterday, Sandler, 51, stressed his gratitude to the stations for "their years of support and loyalty" and said fans "may have misinterpreted something I said on Facebook about how I may be in the market for another job."

But he also said "there have been some conversations" with management about how they want to cover traffic. Although he describes fans' concern as "premature," he also has prominent links on his Facebook page to the "Keep Detour Dave on the Air" page set up by a friend.

I was honest, but discrete and always positive about the station. This was the middle ground that I thought made sense.

I also pursued every job opportunity in case things didn't turn around. WMAR-TV had an opening for an early-morning traffic reporter, and they were happy to audition me. I dragged myself to the station, fully expecting them to tell me that I didn't look well enough to be on the air. They were right. As I laboriously climbed the stairs to the studio, I knew I couldn't handle the 4 a.m. wake up or being on TV. They graciously let me complete the audition, but we all knew the outcome before the cameras rolled. I also responded to leads for corporate spokesmen, but nothing came through. The truth was that I was in no shape to resume full-time work. I still needed a good month to build some strength and lung capacity.

So I clung to hope that the meeting with Dave Hill and Merrie would go well. Six weeks after her call, the three of us gathered in Dave's office. I was glad it had taken that long to arrange because I wanted to look and sound as robust as I could. My voice was still thin but I had put on a little weight and was in much better shape than when she and I had spoken.

The first words out of Dave's mouth were exactly what I needed and wanted to hear. "Dave," he said, "I think there's been a misunderstanding." He continued, "We always wanted you back and have a plan." They offered me 100 hours a month of on-air time between noon and 4 p.m., with fill-ins during other day parts as needed. My start date was March 20, which gave me a few more weeks to regain my mojo. I sensed that Dave was genuinely happy to make the offer. Merrie, too, warmly welcomed me back. If she felt any discomfort at being overruled in front of me she didn't show it. I accepted, and left the station ecstatic.

I admit to feeling confused about why they changed their minds, or why Merrie called me if the decision wasn't final. Those questions have never been answered, and I've never pursued it. I can only speculate about the conversations that may have occurred during my hospitalization. Perhaps management felt that they'd been down this road with me and could not risk the uncertainty. Maybe it was purely financial. Maybe Dave Hill left the final call 'til he saw and heard me. Perhaps Merrie overstepped, or the fan response was more heated than they'd expected. Whatever the reasons, they wanted me back on the air, and that was all I needed to know. Full-time would have been better, but this was a great start.

People have asked me whether I ever feel bitter about the way the situation was handled. My answer is a resounding "NO," and I mean it. WBAL stood by me when I was at my lowest. Their loyalty and generosity was remarkable, and I'll never forget it. I view this episode as Dave characterized it: a misunderstanding. I'm now going on 30 years with them, and it remains the best job in the business.

DETERMINATION

28. THE OLD JOB JUST ISN'T THE SAME

My start date, March 20th, was set, and I couldn't wait to get back behind the mic. Until then I concentrated on strengthening my vocal quality and lung capacity. I didn't want to sound choppy or breathy, so I spent extra time each day on my breathing exercises – I was like an athlete training for my first marathon, and I was determined to have a respectable showing.

When I walked into the studio for my first shift since Thanksgiving, I had some butterflies, I'll admit—mostly about how I sounded. Every other aspect of the job was like riding a bike. I sat down and started pedaling. "Traffic and weather on the 5's … I'm WBAL's Detour Dave Sandler." My intro and sign-off were part of my on-air identity, and it felt empowering to say them again.

I got many calls that afternoon from loyal fans welcoming me back and saying how much they had missed hearing my voice. There was "Jim from Bel Air" on line 1, "Bowie out of Annapolis" on line 2. They were two of many regular callers who alerted me to problems on area roadways. Some listeners wanted to say hi, others asked where I had been. As had been my policy during my convalescence, I provided no details. The parting line was, "I had a little health detour, but I'm feeling great. Thanks for calling!"

Those four hours went smoothly and flew by. My voice may not have been its strongest, but I was broadcasting and my listeners were supportive. I couldn't wait to put on my headphones the next day.

My new 12-4 p.m. shift was much easier than the morning or evening rush hours, so I had time to collect myself between reports. There wasn't much action on the roads, I didn't have to get up at 4:30 a.m., and I was home for dinner with the family at a reasonable hour. My only complaint was my new status as an hourly employee. Prior to this absence, BAL had paid me a full-time salary; now I was compensated only for the hours I worked, and I was down to about 40% of my previous schedule. Doing what I loved was wonderful, but the 60% pay cut was causing us a host of financial problems.

The downturn in our personal economy wasn't due just to cutbacks at BAL. The recession was hurting everyone's pocketbook, so the weddings and parties that had filled my weekends were less frequent and less lavish. Thanks to Google Earth and other GPS services, the aerial photography business had run aground. Suddenly our books had a lot more debits than assets, but our monthly obligations remained: the mortgage, utilities, cell phones, car payments, college tuition and groceries. We were experiencing the same squeeze affecting so many American families, and for the first time since we were struggling newlyweds, we had to prioritize and control our spending.

For years I'd enjoyed generous compensation from BAL and had two side businesses that generated a decent amount of income. We didn't worry about money because we'd never had a reason to. We were used to a certain lifestyle – not extravagant, but very comfortable. Seemingly overnight, we went from living well to living on the edge. We were broke. We could talk around that fact or try to deny it, but it was true. Everything about our finances had changed and we had to, too. We knew that all non-essential spending had to go; if it affected any friendships adversely, then those folks weren't our friends. If we tried to live beyond our means, the lie and our debt would mushroom. We had to say without shame, "This is who we are, and this is what we can afford." After much soul searching, we decided that living authentically and honestly trumped everything else. We also knew we had to implement practical strategies if we were going to reverse the slide.

Jody immediately announced her plan to return to work. She'd taken time off when the kids were younger and had some medical issues that made it difficult to hold a 9-5 office job. Now, given my pay cut, she was determined to contribute to the bottom line. Her twin, Alisa, mentioned an opening for a bookkeeper in the podiatry office where she worked. Jody had ample experience working in medical offices but none specifically as a bookkeeper. Somehow she talked her way into the job and spent five to six hours a day for the next month teaching herself the billing software, codes and procedures.

In addition to learning a new skill set, working and taking care of me and the house, she took command of the entire situation. She had so much on her plate, yet she was always willing to do more if it would help me to heal. This was a huge gift to me because it enabled me to focus on regaining strength and getting through my shift each day. Jody is naturally good at taking charge; her ability to see a situation for what it is and to do what needs to be done without complaining are just two of the many things I love about her. If Larry the Cable Guy hadn't said "Git 'er done" first, I'm sure Jody would have coined the phrase. She is my perfect complement. I couldn't have gotten through any of this without her.

Our kids did what they could to pitch in. Brooks, who was living in an off-campus apartment, volunteered to move home, enabling us to eliminate another big monthly expense. He worked part-time while attending Towson University and refused to take any money from us. Our daughter, Alix, was already working and self-supporting.

All of this helped, but the gaping hole in our finances reminded me of my chest wall: we needed a complete rebuild.

We were lucky to have wonderful friends and family who rallied around us. Some offered financial assistance, but we felt very uncomfortable borrowing money from them. Adding to our debt didn't seem like a smart strategy. We did, grudgingly, accept a loan from my mom and step-dad to tide us over until we had a long-term plan. We knew we needed one but had no idea how to go about creating one.

My good friend, Joe Weinberg, and his wife Debs, who were deeply involved with Jewish Family Services (JFS), suggested that we make an appointment. JFS is a non-profit agency that offers emergency financial assistance, career counseling, and many other services to those in need. At first I was resistant. I felt embarrassed and like a failure—I had always been the breadwinner, and while it may be old-fashioned, it was a point of pride for me that I could support my family. If Jody wanted to work, great, but I hated that she *had* to work because of my condition. I wanted to believe that agencies like JFS were for other people who had hit rock bottom financially. But as the red ink spread, Jody and I realized that we were now those "other people." Our bank balance didn't begin to cover our bills. Once we admitted that to ourselves, it became easier to swallow our pride and make an appointment.

While I went to Hopkins for some follow-up tests, Jody met with a JFS financial counselor and took Alix with her for support. The counselor ushered them into an office with a large window; Jody recalled looking out the window and thinking that the people in the parking lot below were enjoying their day "while I'm in here asking for help to keep food on the table and gas in my car." Jody confessed to the counselor that she was shocked at how quickly our financial circumstances had changed, and embarrassed that we hadn't planned well enough for such an event.

He was understanding and an excellent listener. He reviewed our monthly expenses against income and said he would continue working with us to restructure our debt and manage a budget. Jody left the appointment with gift cards so she could go grocery shopping. She told me, "I remember leaving there feeling so relieved that someone was going to help. They made us feel so comfortable and allowed us to leave with our dignity."

That night, and for many nights to come, we had painful heart-to-hearts about our situation. The more we talked, the more we realized that what happened to us could happen to anyone. None of us can predict all of life's unexpected turns, and we'd certainly had more than our share over the previous two years. We should have been better prepared, but in hindsight … the stories of people who lost everything because of a catastrophic illness were as common as pennies. Instead of feeling self-conscious about it, we said, "Let's embrace it and be thankful that help is out there. We're in this together and we will get through it together. We're not victims. We own it and we'll fix it. I'm regaining my health, you're working, the kids are fine … we have a lot to be grateful for."

As I look back on that period of coming to terms with our money woes, I think a great deal about the issue of control. I'd had none over my illnesses. I got cancer, got treated, and my medical problems festered silently over the next 20+ years. It was a snowflake that turned into an avalanche without my being aware of it. In the case of our finances, everything we'd spent in the past had been in our control; how much or little we'd saved was on us, and every step we took from that point on was in our hands alone. How we acted, how we felt, what we changed … and that was gratifying in ways I didn't expect.

Yes, we felt some guilt about not saving more. The positive was that we could cut up the credit cards, cut out the restaurant meals and drive our cars into the ground. We could be honest about our status. We could say no and feel empowered instead of embarrassed. When Jody and I started looking at our circumstances in that light, we realized that we could rebuild and come back stronger. We could learn to live within our means, whatever they were, and to adjust as needed. In some respects, this come-uppance enabled us to establish greater financial security in the long term. Jody's going back to work renewed her self-confidence and her sense of contribution to the family's finances. My kids gained greater independence. We all learned that there is no shame in reaching out.

These epiphanies didn't come overnight, but in time we began to see the value in what we had lost, because it helped us gain so much wisdom.

REINVENT

29. BACK AT WBAL AT LAST

Between traffic reporting, Jody's job, my DJ gigs, and assistance from JFS, we were squeaking by, but just barely. JFS offered career counseling, so even though I'd done nothing but traffic for my entire career, I attended group and individual sessions. I was amazed to see how many other middle-aged Americans were laid off or displaced by technology.

It wasn't just one-track guys like me, but professionals from virtually every industry. The recession was killing so many people, even those with outstanding skills and experience. I suppose there was some small comfort in knowing I wasn't alone, but at the end of every session I came to the same conclusion: Detour Dave was not equipped to veer off the broadcasting path. I appreciated all the help and advice, but this was my talent. At age 48, accounting or engineering was not in my future.

I decided that the best way to move forward was to enhance what I knew best. I laid out a two-pronged strategy to increase my hours on the air and to pump up the DJ business. Every few weeks I'd stick my head in Dave Hill's office and ask if there was more I could do. He'd always say, "You sound great, Dave. Keep it up!" It was nice to hear, but it wasn't helping the Sandlers' bottom line. Nonetheless, I continued to show my interest because I never knew when something might change. I wanted management to know that I was a team player who loved being on the air and was always ready to do more. Throwing in the towel was never a consideration.

Still, it was hard to contain my frustration over working only four hours a day. Jim Russ handled the 5 a.m. - noon shift, I did mid-day, and Tamara Nelson, who'd been a fill-in while I was recuperating, covered 4-8 p.m.; typically, a station would have two reporters splitting the day around the morning and evening rush hours. Tamara and I both felt shortchanged by the shared shift. We were both good reporters, and we both needed a bigger paycheck. But Dave Hill wasn't making any moves for the moment, so we remained in limbo for a while longer.

Tamara and I spoke often and openly about the situation, and we were in complete agreement that three people were doing the work of two. We knew that, eventually, one of us would have to go. She acknowledged that my longevity and fan base gave me a leg up on the job. To protect herself and create new professional possibilities she began studying for her real estate license. No one in management ever said it, but she and I inferred that the station viewed her as insurance if I got sick again. But I was well now. I suppose that, out of a sense of fairness to her, Dave was trying to be Solomon-like and split the baby. It didn't work for the women in the Bible, and it wasn't working for us.

With that situation static, I focused on the DJ side, with the goal of forging partnerships with some of the catering operations around town. I developed more marketing tools to get my name in front of more industry people. I ran ads, created a new brochure, and met with caterers, photographers, party planners and sales execs, but nothing much came from those efforts. The entire industry was struggling, and everyone who provided party-related services was scrambling for business.

I decided to step way out of my comfort zone by attending a meeting of the National Association of Catering Executives (NACE), a monthly dinner/speaker/networking event for everyone who touches the party industry. I say it was out of my comfort zone for two reasons: prior to this, I hardly had to network to get business. The cachet of hiring Detour Dave for a party had always been enough to keep me booked months in advance. And even though I can work a crowd, I'm not a natural-born schmoozer one-on-one. But I plastered a smile on my face, worked the room, and made small talk. I exchanged a fair number of business cards, but the uptick in bookings was negligible.

That period was disheartening. I was so eager to work. I felt that I was doing all the right things, but I had no control over the national economy or personnel issues at the station. The only thing I could control was my attitude, and I tried to stay positive in spite of all the dead ends. Our JFS counselor was a fantastic cheerleader who never let me give up on myself. We met for an update each month, and I loved spending time with him. It didn't hurt that he was a regular BAL listener and Detour Dave fan. He encouraged me to hang in there and assured Jody and me that they would help us get through this rough patch. They kept their word. We will never forget the support, financial and emotional, that they gave to us when we really needed a boost.

For a few more months the split shift routine continued. Then, as happens so often in broadcasting, BAL changed the chain of command. The News Director at WBAL-TV, Michelle Butt, assumed Dave Hill's duties at the radio station, making the entire news operation one seamless entity. I knew Michelle and had always found her very approachable. A few weeks after she took over I requested a meeting. I wanted to make sure that she knew my health was good and to assess her thoughts about the split shift.

During the meeting I carefully expressed my desire for more hours and assured her that I was up to the task. Her response was refreshing and validating. She said, "Dave, you have a lot of equity here at the station. Everyone knows Detour Dave. You're synonymous with traffic in Baltimore. We need to maximize this. Give me a couple of weeks and I'll get back to you." I left the meeting feeling that Michelle had heard me and recognized my value to the station. It was positive, but I had to bide my time.

A couple of weeks went by and, as promised, Michelle called me into her office to announce that my new shift would be from 9 a.m. to 3 p.m. starting the following week. She thought that my personality would mesh with the two talk show hosts who were on during the day. She expected me to deliver the "accurate information with the off-the-cuff humor that had made [me] a mainstay for more than 25 years." Jim would continue taking care of the two rushes. I was thrilled. My hours had just increased by 50%—not full-time, but significantly better. I shook her hand and thanked her repeatedly for putting her trust in me.

I didn't need to ask how the rest of the story would play out. I had a regular gig and Jim had the morning and evening rush, so Tamara was out. I wanted to call her but knew it wasn't my place until Michelle talked to her. When Tamara called me that evening, I was ready to offer condolences. Before I could speak she said, "Dave, I'm so relieved it's over." I was too, and I was grateful that she handled the decision so graciously and professionally. We spoke for some time and ended on a friendly note. Tamara continues to use her mellifluous voice doing voice-overs and is brokering real estate.

Most of us have faced professional situations in which a colleague becomes a roadblock, and we have to decide how we're going to handle it. In my situation with Tamara, it was simply a matter of too many cooks. She never did anything to harm me, and I was on guard constantly about not becoming the saboteur. I wanted my job back, but I did not want to do or say anything that would cast Tamara in a negative light. I hoped that management would give me the hours because of my talent and ability, period. My goal, as always, was to behave in an ethical manner and earn the position. Gaining an advantage based on anything but merit is no advantage in the long run. Trying to cover up your incompetence is exhausting. The person who shepherds and protects you today may be gone tomorrow, and the next boss will be on to your shortcomings in short order.

Of course if a colleague is conniving to get you in trouble, it's easy to justify taking the low road. It's natural to feel angry and want to push back. But I believe that this is the perfect time for some self-advocacy. It's much more productive than backstabbing, because your actions can never come back to haunt you, unlike your tormenter's. Speaking ill of others always reflects poorly on your character, and it implies that your boss doesn't see what you're seeing. That's tremendously off-putting to someone who has worked his/her way up to a management position. Never assume a lack of awareness; your boss may not be in a position to act, but that doesn't mean s/he doesn't get it.

A better strategy is to communicate to management at appropriate intervals that you're interested and ready for more, as I did with Dave Hill. Don't be a pest – time your drop in's – but do find ways to talk about projects you're working on or ideas you have that will benefit the company. Being a problem-solver is an effective way to show your value without diminishing someone else.

Taking the high road isn't always easy, but you'll never have trouble sleeping at night.

INTEGRITY

30. PROFESSIONAL LIFE LESSONS

So what did I learn from this crazy last chapter of my life? As a professional, I've always tried to abide by some simple rules based on time-tested fundamentals: honesty, integrity, kindness, hope, trust and discretion. Here are my guideposts:

NEVER BURN A BRIDGE. In more than one professional situation I had the opportunity to set a bonfire and chose not to. A contact is worth preserving because you never know when someone can help you and vice versa. Airing your grievances publicly or slamming doors on your way out is childish and never in your best interest. You may have a moment of satisfaction but venting won't put money in the bank or bread on the table. Maintaining positive relationships is vital to a successful professional life. Complain as much as you want to your spouse or best friend, but otherwise, zip it.

NEVER GIVE UP HOPE. A decision is final only when the locks are changed or they call the undertaker. Ask for a meeting and specifics about why your future may be in jeopardy. Bring examples of contributions you've made that your boss may have overlooked. You may have to move on, but you'll have done most of the legwork to update your resume.

IDENTIFY YOUR GOVERNING PRINCIPLES. What do you stand for? How do you conduct yourself? Do you think before you speak? Do you feel entitled to say whatever is on your mind? How do you think others perceive you? These might sound like simple, even silly, questions, but they have a purpose. Most of us don't take the time to establish a creed of personal behavior. We react in the moment instead of adhering to a set of principles that will keep us out of trouble. Preparation is invaluable, whether you're making a major presentation or presenting yourself on a daily basis. Sit down with a pen and paper and write down the qualities you admire most in others. Ask yourself if they apply to you, and answer honestly. Changing behavior isn't easy, but if you start with specific words, like "honesty," "integrity," "kindness," "listening," or others that appeal to you, you'll have goals to aim for.

FIND THE BALANCE BETWEEN SELF-INTEREST AND A LOCK-OUT. When you think you've lost your job, or are about to, what do you do? The first step is to peel back the emotion and write down the facts of the case. Make an honest assessment; maybe it's not as bad as you think. If it is, or it makes you feel better, start looking discreetly. Facebook has incredible reach, but it's not the best place to post your resume until you're officially out. You're not just communicating with your circle, but with all of those overlapping circles – and the HR director may be in one. Once you post it, you can't retract it. Personal inquiries to people you trust is a better first step.

At the same time, do not sit passively waiting for the axe to fall. If all signs point to your dismissal, be proactive. Update your resume and all of your online professional profiles. Make a list of potential contacts. And when you get the pink slip, negotiate for the best severance you can unless you've been let go on grounds. Then it's time for a thorough reassessment of what you did wrong and a plan to make sure it never happens again.

NOBODY IS PERFECT – INCLUDING YOU. Cut people

some slack. You don't know what happened to make them irritable or impatient. Give everyone the benefit of the doubt. It will soften any resentment you feel. Make generosity your go-to response and save the anger for something that matters. Like a heart attack or cancer.

KNOCK THE CHIP OFF YOUR SHOULDER. Are you one of those people who always feel you're getting a raw deal? That the world is conspiring to marginalize you? Get over it. Step back and assume that whatever just happened has nothing to do with you. If someone is intentionally working against you, you'll see a pattern soon enough. Otherwise, understand that the earth doesn't revolve around you. Most of us are too busy to plot. Put a smile on your face and leave the chip behind. Acting like a victim is the fastest way to become one.

ADVOCATE FOR YOURSELF. BUT LEAVE THE TRUMPET AT HOME. Let's say that a pattern emerges. A co-worker continually steals all the credit or tries to make you look bad. Or let's say that your mutual boss doesn't seem to pay the same attention to your efforts. It's time to be proactive, without casting anyone else in a bad light. Communicate with your supervisor about what you're working on. Discuss what's going well and ask for advice about what isn't. Ignore the schemer and assume that your boss sees exactly what you're seeing. If your colleague crosses a line, take it up the chain. Otherwise, trust that his/her unhelpful behavior will catch up with them eventually. It usually does.

If your boss just doesn't seem to like you as much, look at your own behavior and try to figure out why. Sometimes it's just chemistry, and there's not much you can do about it. Or look at your colleague's behavior. Maybe s/he needs more encouragement to stay on track. Maybe your boss secretly appreciates you for NOT being so needy. Assume nothing. As long as you're doing your job well and getting positive performance reviews, let it slide.

EXERCISE THE 24-HOUR RULE. A friend once shared this advice from a boss, and I think it sums up all of these lessons in a simple technique. When something happens that makes your blood boil, say nothing. Walk away. Wait 24 hours. Then imagine what you will say to the person who angered you. If you feel the adrenaline rush and your blood pressure shoots up, say nothing. Wait another 24 hours. Repeat until you can speak without feeling physically angry. Then, and only then, are you ready to have a calm conversation. If you feel the anger rise while you're speaking, excuse yourself with, "Let's continue this later. I do not think we are being productive." Repeat until you can talk or the storm passes.

SUCCESS

31. POST SCRIPT

WBAL recently implemented round-the-clock traffic reports to cover incidents in real time – as we all know, in a crowded metro area accidents can happen at any time. Jim Russ continues with the morning rush and the station contracts with a traffic service to handle the off-peak hours. I deliver my traffic reports from 3-7:15 p.m., Monday through Friday. Those hours are perfect – I do *not* miss those 4 a.m. wake ups. The pace is fast as we try to help countless drivers in the Baltimore region make it home for dinner. I'm sure the commuters wish the pace was fast for them as well, but that's rare. I think my voice sounds strong, although my lungs will never be where they were. I'm giving 100% to my 70% capacity and striving to be my best, regardless of any physical limitations.

It's wonderful to be doing the job I love once again. As always, my listeners are loyal and supportive; they were a big motivation for writing this book. I hope that anyone who faces a major life challenge, health related or otherwise, will find comfort and inspiration from my crazy ride.

Most of my weekends are booked entertaining at private parties and charitable and corporate functions. As the economy has improved, individuals and companies are throwing more parties, which is great for the business. I enjoy emceeing now as much as I did when I started with John Patti a few decades ago. I'm getting smarter, too: I now employ some younger talent to lug the equipment. It's amazing how fresh I feel without the backaches that accompany the set-ups and breakdowns. I've been named the exclusive entertainment provider for Michael's 8th Avenue, a popular Baltimore party venue, and am adding new DJ talent to the Traffic Jams roster.

My health will always be a concern. The radiation will continue to have unforeseen side effects because I'm part of the first generation of long-term Hodgkin's survivors. The medical community continues to learn from our experience and refines treatments all the time. Unfortunately for me, my heart and lungs have been scarred and that is not reversible. But I have amazing doctors who know how to handle my complex case. I trust them with every decision – they have never let me down and have never given up on me. They continue to try new therapies to keep me in the best possible shape. I'm not perfect, but I'm content. As long as I give 100% in whatever capacity I have, I'm satisfied.

I'm looking forward to many new and exciting chapters on the road ahead. I believe that it will continue to be a fantastic ride, no matter what detours come my way.

ACKNOWLEDGEMENTS

To Jody: you support me unconditionally and are the person I can lean on for every-thing. You are my life, my love and best friend.

To Alix: my first born and wonderful daughter. I love watching you grow up into a smart and beautiful women. You are doing great things. Continue to pursue your dreams.

To Brooks: my son and favorite person to watch, talk and enjoy my passion of sports with. You are destined for greatness.

To Mom: thank you for your wisdom and guidance. You planted the seed for my success and always were there for me every step of the way.

To Dad: I miss you. You would have been proud of what your boys have accomplished. Thanks for the early attitude lessons and teaching me how to hit that little white ball so well.

To Doug: growing up along side of you was easy. You have always been a great brother and watched out for me. Our parallel careers keep pushing me to greatness.

To Marty: you have treated me like a son from my days in elementary school. Thanks for taking care of all of us, but especially mom. You are incredible.

To Rich and Nancy: I have always felt you are my biological brother and sister. I'm so fortunate to have you in my life.

To Alisa and Nancy: you have helped me understand what a close knit family is all about. Your support is amazing and your love for Jody is what makes her so special.

To David and Steven: you have been like brothers to me. You are there for me when I call on you. You are unsung hero's.

To Rick and Joey: my closest friends and best athletic partners. I love knowing you are always there for me. Friendships are forever.

To Skip: my great friend and sports buddy. I know you are only a phone call away. I wish you lived closer.

To Mike Herr: thanks for bringing me onto the team. Softball may have saved my life and you being there reassured that. I'm so grateful.

To Scott Katzen: your friendship is treasured. Your ability to stay calm under the circumstances has allowed me to live. Words cannot express my gratitude.

To Larry, Rob, Jon, Troy and Robbie: our friendships will last a lifetime. You guys are great.

To Dorrie: your ability to express my feelings into words has made this book shine. Let's do it again sometime. You are truly gifted.

To Boh, Teddy, Buddy, Hootie and Sammie: the licks and wags kept me going every day. You are truly this man's best friend.

To my extended family: thank you for all the support I get each and everyday. You lift me up and make me feel special.

To my doctors and caretakers: I have the best medical staff in the world. I'm so fortunate to live in an area which has the resources to keep me healthy. I'm a lucky guy.

To WBAL and 98 Rock: I have the best co-workers a guy could ever dream of. You have made me a better broadcaster and a better man.

To my listeners: you have inspired me to write this book. Your undying support is felt everyday. I promise to keep moving you through each detour.

To Kevin and Apprentice House Press: I appreciate your confidence in me and for allowing me to tell my story.

To all of my relatives and friends who have passed away: thank you for touching my life and watching over me. I will see you again.

—

As they saying goes "it takes a village to raise a child" well it takes a village to help a person recover and heal. We were so fortunate to have that village. Their were so many people that called, drove us to the hospital, went foodshopping, sent in meals, let the dogs out and so much more. I may forget a few so I'm sorry, but the biggest supporters were our families. My sisters Alisa and Nancy and their husbands Steven and Dave (another Dave). I couldn't have gotten through any of this without my dear friend Barbara Getlan. The best nurse ever and she helped us coordinate things every step of the way . Their are not enough thanks you that I can say to her, but thank you. My other besties, Jamie Verrecchio, Darla Lansman Gwen Hirsch, Linda Nachimson, Wanda Sizter, Rita Shemer and my cousin Dorrie Anshel. These girls kept me going day after day. We all powered through the journey together. It makes a big difference who is there to support you. I had the best team. Thanks to my kids, Alix and Brooks too for stepping up to the plate in more ways then one. And last but not least Dr Scott Katzen and Dr Michael Herr for saving my husband. I will be forever grateful that you both are in our lives.

—*Jody Sandler*

ABOUT THE AUTHORS

Detour Dave Sandler has been delivering traffic reports to Baltimore/Washington area on WBAL and 98 Rock since 1986. He is also the president of Detour Dave Inc, which operates an entertainment company and provides aerial photography for commercial and residential real-estate. Since the release of *Taking a Detour*, he has added inspirational and motivational speaking to his list of professions. Dave and his wife Jody live in Reisterstown, Maryland. They have two children, Alix and Brooks.

Dorrie Anshel spent ten years in corporate communications before starting a freelance writing business. She has written for all media for large national corporations, start-ups, and non-profits across a variety of industries. This collaboration with Dave is her first; she looks forward to helping other people share their compelling stories. She lives with her family in Ocean View, Delaware.

Apprentice House is the country's only campus-based, student-staffed book publishing company. Directed by professors and industry professionals, it is a nonprofit activity of the Communication Department at Loyola University Maryland.

Using state-of-the-art technology and an experiential learning model of education, Apprentice House publishes books in untraditional ways. This dual responsibility as publishers and educators creates an unprecedented collaborative environment among faculty and students, while teaching tomorrow's editors, designers, and marketers.

Outside of class, progress on book projects is carried forth by the AH Book Publishing Club, a co-curricular campus organization supported by Loyola University Maryland's Office of Student Activities.

Eclectic and provocative, Apprentice House titles intend to entertain as well as spark dialogue on a variety of topics. Financial contributions to sustain the press's work are welcomed. Contributions are tax deductible to the fullest extent allowed by the IRS.

To learn more about Apprentice House books or to obtain submission guidelines, please visit www.apprenticehouse.com.

Apprentice House
Communication Department
Loyola University Maryland
4501 N. Charles Street
Baltimore, MD 21210
Ph: 410-617-5265 • Fax: 410-617-2198
info@apprenticehouse.com • www.apprenticehouse.com